THE GLIMMER OF LIGHT

SUMMER BREEZE

Contents

———

DEDICATION

I normally dedicate my books to my one true legacy.

For Blaise, Westin and Colton.

Not this time.

For Westin, Colton, and Blaise.

Because Westin is tired of always being in the middle and Colton is tired of being listed last as the youngest.

Meanwhile, Blaise is protesting his birthright.

For my husband Buddha Man aka Corey.

Who drove me completely crazy with some of the best advice anyone has ever given me.

One day at a time. I repeat, One day at a time.

And that cold pizza is actually pretty good.

To my Mom Pamela.

For teaching me that an arrow can only be shot by pulling it backward.

So, when life is dragging you back It's going to launch you into something great.

Look Mom, I made it!

To the Frenchie's and the Irish Water Spaniels.

Who were no help at all and kept this book from getting done sooner than later.

And For teaching me to kick grass over that shit and move on.

To those who inspired it and will not read it. To everyone who wonders if I am writing about them. I am.

To all my haters, thank you for keeping me motivated, famous, and for being my biggest fans!

Always respect your haters for they are the only ones who think you're better than them.

Haters

H: Having

A: Anger

T: Towards

E: Everyone

R: Reaching

S: Success

There are many intriguing queries about several species in life's large landscape of mysteries. One is whether or not the Polyphemus Moth knows its impending beauty after it emerges from its silky cocoon comfort zone. The topic has been pondered, whether the Moth is completely aware of its gorgeous, violet and gold, owl-eyed wings that will soon reveal themselves or do they present themselves to the moth as a glorious divine surprise. The Polyphemus derives its name from the Greek myth of the cyclops Polyphemus. This one-eyed goliath man was the son of Poseidon and Thoosa. Polyphemus is vividly described in great detail within Homer's Odyssey. The name means abounding in beautiful songs and extraordinary legends. Like the myth of Polyphemus, this striking moth can eat eighty-six thousand times its weight in a matter of only two months. Although they appear to be extremely dangerous as the eyes on their wings glare back at their enemies, they are one hundred percent harmless and bland with their defenses. They are not harmless prior to them coming into their wings, giving them the best chance at spreading their chalky textured wings in the future. As bright lime green caterpillars, they are mildly toxic to humans. They present a stinging sensation with a prickly warning when bothered. This would make complete sense due to their extremely short life span. The Polyphemus Moth only survives in all its beauty and glory for a mere minuscule week lifespan. These moths give off a false sense of fear to other insects and humans alike. The imaginative eyes that stare back from the rearmost position of their wings breach into the utter soul as a warning to back away smoothly to not draw attention from the eyes. They lead everything and everyone that surrounds them to believe they are deadly when in fact, they are undamaging and nontoxic.

CHAPTER 1

Just like the Polyphemus Moth, Penelope had put on a false sense of threat and bravery throughout her life. She was like a Polyphemus Moth going through her tragic chosen life with a pretense of her courage and strength. She would justify this strength in ways that would convince even the strongest people that she was something to be respected. In all actuality, she was putting on nothing but grand facades and was scared to death at every season of change. Someday, Penelope unexpectedly would be able to marvel in her own ravishing beauty. Like the moth with its glamorized owl-eyed wings, she too would be astonished in the unwavering strength and appealing courage she unknowingly had her entire life. Penelope never immersed out of what she presumed was her secured and safeguarded chrysalis. Out of fear, she remained tightly wrapped frightened of the pain and the impending truth about her unpleasant situation she would have to face. Soon,

Penelope would finally be able to peel back the layers of her swaddled cloak of protection and soar to unimaginable heights into the celestial majestic horizon.

She looked feeble and unstable as she stood there, a bloody mess from just having taken a vicious blow to the brim of her eyebrow from Smitty. The blood streaming down the side of her head from being slammed against the weathered red bench in their garden was pooling on the ground in front of her. One bright red droplet at a time would fall from her cheek and join the puddle of despise below. Not much remained of Smitty, Penelope's husband, the Fallen Angel, in that Tulip Garden. That fall day in that Nebraska garden, the dusty remains of a defeated Demon from a malevolent world, displayed itself in front of Penelope and the Summers. Dean, Heather's husband, the Seer, had done the difficult and unwaning task of defeating a very powerful Demon. Dean had stopped Smitty from the completion of a dangerous and wicked blue print of ruin. He had killed Smitty with Heather's Grandmother's divine triple-edged Archangel Blade. It was a fight-or-flight situation, and Dean never backed down from a fight. A thin layer of ashy-looking filth covered a once splendid lush part of the Smith's yard, which was now the only evidence of Smitty walking among the people. On top of the grime were a few of Smitty's charcoaled black feathers, leaving their ominous omen signs on Earth just as they did on Heather's Wedding Day and in the ICU waiting room after Penelope's stroke. A Demon that was never meant to be among the living. Smitty was a Demon who Shined with evil intent and all-inclusive ruin. He was once an Angel that followed Satan into battle against the Heavens. When Satan lost that battle, he tortured all the Angels that had followed him. He tortured them so horrifically that all their purity and goodness were taken from them, leaving them with only hatred and malice. A demon's only chance to return to glorified Heaven was to take possession of a person on Earth. This Demon took over Smitty as a young child and became the Fallen Angel known as Smitty. Demons prey on the sorrowful souls of humans that have lost their paths to righteousness. Where there is good, there will always be evil. Evil cannot exist without good, whereas good can exist without evil.

It is not a codependent relationship like the Devil and Demons want people to believe. Smitty was sexually abused as a young child by a Catholic Priest. This made him despise the church and everything it stood for in his mind. This was the reasoning behind Smitty not wanting anything to do with the church despite his Mother Clementine's wishes. Clementine was unaware of the abuse until it was too late, and the crime on Smitty's soul had been committed. One gloomy Sunday afternoon after a church service. They arrived home, all going about their regular Sunday routines. His siblings went to their bedrooms to change out of their Sunday best. Clementine and Cletus went straight to their garden to pick some freshly home-grown vegetables for dinner. Smitty, on the other hand, went directly to the kitchen in their two-story home. He turned on the stove top, placed all the cloth pot holders on the burning red coils, and set their house on fire. He walked downstairs to his bedroom and sat on the end of the bed. He heard the smoke alarms start to go off and could smell the kitchen engulfed in flames. The smoke seeped under the crack at the bottom of the door and started to fill his bedroom with black grit. This set his smoke alarm off, screaming above the door, but Smitty didn't budge from the end of his bed. This was his cry out for help. Due to the sexual abuse, he was terrified about confessing sin to his parents Clementine and Cletus. He was led to believe he was the one sinning, not his abuser. His abuser put the fear of God into him, literally, since he was a man of the cloak and was to be respected. Smitty could hear Clementine and Cletus calling 911 and yelling for all the children to get outside. The house was on fire. Suddenly, Smitty's bedroom door swings open, and Cletus storms in, snatching Smitty up. Cletus throws his seventy-five-pound son over his shoulder like a sack of potatoes, sprinting towards the basement door to escape. The fire fighters arrived and put out the kitchen fire slowly but surely, as all the nosey and curious neighbors looked on and peeked out their windows. It had destroyed the entire kitchen and the dining room by the time the flames were extinguished. The firefighters could not tell Cletus and Clementine what caused the kitchen fire, assuming it was bad wiring of an appliance. Of Course, Smitty never revealed to his parents that the fire damage done to their home was masterminded by him intentionally. He never returned to church religiously after the fire that day. He had stopped talking and wouldn't communicate his pain and sorrow with anyone. His family thought he was going through dissociation shock about the house fire and the devastation it left in its path. His family blamed some exaggerated puberty and chalked his new muteness to moodiness. They attributed his new mute state of mind to the fire trauma, so he was allowed to stay home on Sundays with Cletus, who never attended church. Smitty would make homemade pizza for his family to come home to after Sunday service in their brand-new kitchen with all new appliances. This very dejected, melancholy little boy reluctantly turned towards the dark side as a teen under the guidance of the Fallen Angel named Birsha. This Demon was starting his possession, seeing a weakness and sorrow in Smitty that would consume his soul if not dealt with head-on. Birsha, The Fallen Angel, was pure evil. The name Birsha in Hebrew means evil, fitting for the goals this

Demon was trying to achieve. That was Smitty, a pure evil Fallen Angel.

CHAPTER 2

Possession takes years and happens in several stages over an extended period of time. Stage one is Identification. The person cannot tell if their problems are physical, mental, or spiritual. This is a very confusing time for the person, purposedly and perfectly placed by the Demons. The second stage of possession is Escalation. This is where the night terrors reveal themselves in their wicked nature, and the person begins to lose all senses of true reality. Also, all part of the Demon's strategy to make the person feel as though they are losing their mind. The third stage is Domonic Obsession when a physical illness occurs without reasoning or cure for the illness. It can't be explained and is very severe. Stage four is the most terrifying of all the stages. This is the part that becomes unexplainable and spiritually connected. The person is sometimes able to speak in languages they never knew prior. This is called speaking in tongues. The person's pupils in their eyes become snake-like, and they obtain super human strength. Religious artifacts and blessed objects such as Bibles, Rosaries, and Holy Water are all things deeply detested by such a person. These items are some of the divine objects that cause a Demon to become physically ill and make them pale in stature. Sometimes the Demons show off their pure dark evil abilities and create disturbances in the environment around them. People who have been taken all the way through to stage four by a Demon have been known to levitate, defy gravity, and create several doppelgangers. Doppelgangers are shadows of one's self. To duplicate a person's personality is considered becoming their double. The spiritual questions then come into play and are utterly unexplainable since multiple identities are sometimes a very common part of Demon possessions. Several Exorcists have experienced and documented these doppelgangers throughout hundreds of years. Documentations of this go all the way back to 1614. When a child has emotional, sexual, or severe environmental trauma, multiple personality disorders sometimes occur. These are also called dissociative disorders. In non-possession form cases, people do not display their change in identities for extended periods of time. If the frequency of the doppelganger identities increases violently with anger and hatred, it's most likely in a possession stage. These are very similar in characteristics, and Demons are aware of this. They will camouflage their possession stages in ways that Psychologists and Doctors can't explain. The symptoms will intentionally mimic other illnesses or disorders, so the Demon can succeed with the possession and stay under the radar. They have one goal: to get through to stage four without any interruptions and fully take over that person's soul. This is their only option to try to sneak back into Heaven's gate. Many disorders are triggered by extreme levels of stress and uncontrollable emotions, all of which also happen due to a person who is entirely confused while going through the Demon's possession stages. Disorders are also known to be triggered by substances and the situations following their consumption. People are very susceptible to taking substances during extremely desolate, confusing, and misunderstood seasons in their lives. Going through the possession stages would be for sure one of those times. So many unexplainable and unbelievable things happen to a person during a possession. People don't feel comfortable with things that they can't scientifically explain. Most people fear the unknown and prefer to stay in denial about the existence of this evil among them. Some want to live their lives in the cloud they have built for themselves. Admitting to such tragedies and lack of goodness in their world would almost be too much for their minds to comprehend. Possessed people are often times painstakingly led by the Demon to make it look like a substance abuse issue rather than a full-on Demon possession. Demons are gifted the ability to be Chameleons with their ruin and have perfected their crafts by the teachings of Satan himself. How do you think they have gotten away with their sinful schemes for so many centuries? They are overly aware of human strengths and personal weaknesses. This awareness is beyond heightened with abilities to extinguish all happiness inside a person. When a person says they are battling their Demons, this just may be an understatement unknowingly made by that person. Demons eradicate the peace inside a person's soul and replace it with utter doubt. They disconnect the blissfulness and reinstate it with complete uncertainty. They confiscate all pureness and swap it out for loathing. For their goal, isn't only to obtain a spot in Heaven that they have been banished from, but it also is to demolish the chosen person and their soul in the process. Annihilation is what they strive for here on Earth.

CHAPTER 3

Heather slowly and cautiously walked towards Penelope with the Archangel Blade now in her hands. Dean had seen that he would be the one to send Smitty the Fallen Angel back. He had seen the premonitions with his third eye. He knew the outcome, and he knew it would be him. He had shared with his sons his sightings but never with Heather. The outcome would remain the same so that the pain could wait. Dean, Asher, Cruz, and Grayson remain standing still within all their Shine and among their glorifying spectacular wing spans. Now a blood-stained result of her life, Penelope doesn't realize that her daughter, who never walked the Earth, is holding her hand. Heather can see her older sister Autumn holding Penelope's hand with one hand and a Lilac branch in the other. The divine wall of all the Grandparents disappeared, and the only reinforcement remaining was

Autumn, Heather's sister, who she had never met. Autumn gave off spiritual kind heartiness, and she had such a high level of benevolence it almost radiated from her. Heather reached Penelope and saw the relief in her eyes. She had a look of thankfulness and freedom Heather had never seen in her mother's eyes displayed before this moment. Heather turned and saw her three sons and Dean rounding the front of the house, leaving Heather and Her mother, Penelope standing there alone with Autumn. Heather began to tell Penelope that her daughter Autumn was there and was holding her mother's hand. Penelope began to break down. She sits down on the garden bench that had just knocked her unconscious moments before. Penelope's blood remaining on the bench's armrest was evidence of the open skull crack it left on Penelope's head as proof. Penelope started to panic, asking Heather how she would ever explain what happened to Smitty. Heather told her that the best thing she could do was tell everyone he ran off, which would surprise no one if they really knew him. Penelope asked Heather what she was supposed to tell Heather's sister Cassie. Heather recommended that

Penelope try to tell her the absolute truth. Penelope still treated Cassie like a fragile child that would break if ever told the reality about life and its adult issues; of course, Penelope refused. Heather told Penelope it was her place as her mother to try to make Cassie understand. Heather would not be taken seriously since she was never respected within the realms of the Smith family. Smitty and Penelope's attitude towards Heather bled straight into Cassie and her regards about her divine sister, whom she knew nothing about. Heather didn't really expect Penelope to act any other way with Cassie; again, all part of Penelope's spiritual journey, she was to walk alone. Heather felt Cassie would only be concerned with her own wellbeing as usual and wouldn't flinch much about Smitty missing regardless. He was the kind of guy who would just start a new life, and it would be no big deal. Heather told Penelope to rent out their house in Nebraska and move on with her life in another state. Penelope had to start over with her life. She wouldn't be able to sell the property with Smitty's name on it, and not being able to come up with a death certificate, renting it out would be Penelope's only option. Penelope, still doubting herself, became quiet and numb. Smitty's parents, Cletus and Clementine, were gone, and his siblings didn't care for him, so they didn't keep in touch and wouldn't miss him. They would not question his sudden disappearance for a second. His business was in shambles, and there was talk about him folding it up. His clients and his workers would also just chalk it up to way too many tough construction years and harsh Nebraska winters with little to no work. Heather knew that her task was still ahead of her now. Although she was meant to play a role in this assignment, it wasn't hers alone. She was meant to meet Dean the Seer, which was the end result of that meeting. Smitty wasn't her main assignment as she had originally thought. This is why her grandmother loved and approved of Dean so highly when she met him. She knew he would play a grand part in taking down Smitty the Fallen Angel. Her three Shining sons were sent as her reinforcements, and that's just what they remained. Heather was a Guardian Angel with a divine assignment still patiently waiting for her divine intervention.

CHAPTER 4

The sultry Nebraska summer was coming to an end. The Summers and their Frenchies were beyond ready to return to their beach front home on the Oregon coastline. The fully furnished apartment they had rented for the summer in Nebraska never felt like home, but more of a work place they could never punch out of with a time card. They all knew that Penelope would have to find her way on her own and reinvent her life as she knew it. Penelope kept the Holy Water necklace that Heather gave her around her neck. After what she had witnessed, Penelope also thought it was a brilliant idea to never take it off again. Penelope ended up with ten staples in the back of her head from the bench episode and two very dark shiners that constantly reminded her of the asylum she put herself in for far too many decades. She packed up what remained of her life and set out to start a new beginning.

She decided to move to Fargo, North Dakota. Penelope thought it was similar to Nebraska, and she could feel more comfortable with familiar surroundings and the weather she was accustomed to. Long, hot, buggy summers and cold, brutal winters were her cup of tea and jam. Although Fargo was a much larger city than Ashton, Nebraska, she felt at home there. It still had that midwestern small-town feel, with those same midwestern accents. She rented a small apartment, got a job at a local western store, and started healing. Penelope's spiritual journey had finally begun, and she could gain some ground now with Smitty's impending abuse no longer surrounding her. The Summers were never so happy as when they boarded the 757 big jet airliner to head back to the coastline they craved and needed again. The Frenchies adjusted to Nebraska, but they ran straight for the beach when they returned to Oregon. There was a rare environmental occurrence when the Summers returned home. The dynamic duo Brutus and Blue, their French Bulldogs, were stopped in their tracks by suspicious-looking blue jelly-like blobs. There were thousands of Velella Velella jellyfish-like creatures that omit a vibrate blue color. Like their cousins, the jellyfish, they are mystifying and magical looking, but they will sting and are best left alone. This jellyfish-like species forms a large agglomeration on beaches when they wash ashore. They float on the ocean's surfaces their entire life span catching the wind heading for the horizon. They are usually about three inches long and have a rigid-like sail on their backs to help set sail around the oceans. They are called "By-the-Wind-Sailors." As Heather tries to catch up to her Bullies, she sees the shoreline covered in blue. Velella Velella covered the entire beach with a spectacular navy-blue blanket of wonderment and beauty. The shorelines on the coast never stop amazing the Summers. The beach gifts that the ocean delivers for beachcombers were immense and always had a grand surprise waiting for them. The Velella Velella were a nice welcome home greeting for the Summers. It was a long summer with stroke victim Penelope and Smitty's impending doom. The sapphire brilliance was such a nice reprieve. The Summers felt like Velella Vellela themselves, always catching the next summer breeze to take them on their ensuing journeys in life. The Summers were "By-the-Wind-Sailors."

CHAPTER 5

The Summers were unknowingly once again about to be "By-the-Wind-Sailors." Dean worked for the U.S. Department of Coastal Fish and Wildlife Service. The previous spring, the Chinook Salmon season was canceled due to a threat of low spawning among the species. This was due to several years of drought in the surrounding rivers. Dean was asked to head a study about the Chinook "King" Salmon in Alaska. The Chinook Salmon is Alaska's state fish, so there is no better place to fully try to understand the species, its habitats, and spawning trends. Within a few months into the late fall, the Summers found themselves on the way to Nome, Alaska. The Chinook were also found in very low alarming numbers in some places in Alaska, compared to previous years. The King Salmon is the largest Pacific Salmon, usually measuring about thirty-six inches and exceeding thirty-plus pounds.

They spend about five years feeding in the open waters of the vast ocean before returning to spawn in their home freshwater streams and rivers. Dean's new job in Nome, Alaska, was documenting habitat changes and extremely fluctuating Chinook spawning levels. This would bring him to various parts of Alaska to compare dwindling Salmon numbers. This greatly affects the Peninsular Grizzly population in Alaska as well. September is a priority month for the Grizzlies to bulk themselves up on Salmon, preparing themselves for their long months in hibernation. An eight hundred-to-twelve-hundred-pound Grizzly will consume approximately thirty to forty Salmon per day. The bears will digest about one hundred pounds of Salmon a day, or one hundred thousand calories. Nome, Alaska, is located on the Seward Peninsula on Norton Sound of the Bering Sea. Its population is a whopping four thousand people, and it's famous for being the finish line for the Iditarod Trail Sled Dog Race. The Iditarod is a thousand-mile dogsled race that starts in Willow, Alaska, and finishes in Nome. The event is held annually on the first Saturday in March. There's no driving to Nome, for it's not part of

Alaska's road system. The Summers flew to Anchorage and then took an hour and a half flight, one hundred and fifty miles to Nome. Cars are not a necessity in Nome. There are three scenic highways that people rent cars to visit. Usually, this is only done during the summer months. The winters make the road conditions unpassable and too dangerous. Nome has a deep-water seaport used by cargo and cruise ships. The Fish and Wildlife Department found the Summers a beautiful, snow-covered log cabin on the outskirts of Nome. When they landed in their new place in late September, it was Nome Sweet Home. Snow arrives in the early fall most years in Nome, and that year was no exception. They already had record-breaking below-freezing negative temperatures and snowfall. Temperatures are known to dip brisk and frigid -55 below zero on any given day in Nome. The windchill that blows off the Bering Sea hovers over the city. The cabin was fully furnished with log furniture, log beds, and quilts sporting wildlife themes. A large stone fireplace heated the cabin, all with woodcut and corded all by hand. Heather's first thought was of how wonderful Christmas would be in the cabin, how the cabin screamed comforting and warming on long winter nights. Heather could picture the cabin with a roaring fire crackling and a blizzard socking them in for some much-needed winter's rest. The front porch was filled with logs, ready to heat the cabin at a moment's notice. It was an a-frame style log home with enormous windows that displayed breathtaking Bering Sea displays. The Sea seemed to be never-ending and stretched to the distant horizon. The sea is the boundary between the United States and Russia. Which is only about a very short distance of one hundred and sixty miles apart. The Bering Sea roughly resembled a triangle with an apex pointed towards the north. Although it was part of the United States, to the Summers, Nome seemed otherworldly in a multitude of ways. The Sea surrounding Nome is one of Earth's most intense patches of oceans. It is known for being one of the most dangerous bodies of water in the entire world. There are three main reasons why the Bering Sea boasts a real threat and should be taken seriously. Its shallow depths of twelve thousand nine hundred and thirteen feet, volatile weather patterns, and the brutal cold sea temperatures filled with Pacific Sleeper Sharks create the perfect horrifying storm. Nome is a very mysterious nautical city. The city has no highways leading to other cities, towns, or villages. To escape the desolate city, a flight out must be booked, or a trip out on a boat is the only other option. This is one of the reasons why all the disappearances throughout the years in Nome are so peculiar and embedded with complete mystery. No one can leave or return without documentation and the entire town knowing in advance. Missing people are a hot topic of gossip along the Norton Sound. Certain areas on this Earth seem to be magnets for missing individuals with no explanations. Nome is in one of these covert areas that the community called the Alaskan Triangle. This bizarre triangle has witnessed over sixteen thousand mysterious and unexplainable disappearances over the years. During any given year, five hundred to two thousand people go missing in Alaska. Rumors spiral around alien abductions and much more sinister reasons. The Alaskan Triangle is often compared to the Bermuda Triangle with its familiar comparable anomalies and tragedies. The Summers knew about Nome's obscurities, but being four people who Shined and one Seer, let's just say nothing like this petrified them. They had seen Demons and unimaginable evil already arrive in their lives. They all knew that what others like to think is pretend was actually very real and presented itself among them often. What they didn't know was that Nome was going to be no exception to that rule. Evil exists everywhere and among everyone. Evil has no boundaries and thrives in many locations.

CHAPTER 6

Nome sweet home was a new chapter in what would seem like a never-ending story for the Summers. Dean was busy with his work projects for the first few months after arriving in Alaska. He had a passion for helping species continue to thrive, and this would present itself with new challenges that he was always up to taking head-on. He preferred a busy mind in order to calm an anxious soul, all characteristics of a Seer. The Chinook Salmon seem to be decreasing for similar reasons in Alaska, and the project was proving beneficial to the Fish and Wildlife Department. Heather kept herself industrious, making homemade Reindeer ornaments for the locals, which then went viral. She found herself with a company shipping the ornaments around the world. In Nome, the Inupiat Eskimos would be more likely to say they encountered Reindeer rather than Caribou. Although they are considered the same species and can interbreed, the local Inuit Tribes call them all Reindeer instead of Caribou. Food is sometimes near impossible to obtain during Nome's long brutal winter months. It all has to be either flown in by plane or boated in, both a very expensive way to grocery shop. The Inuit hunt Reindeer for meat and use every part of the animal for various supplies and decor. Heather found her supplies among the three Eskimo cultures that would sell her the Reindeer hides for a fair price. She then would cut the hide into leather Reindeer ornaments. She handmade the tiny leather horns and red noses made out of dyed prehistoric walrus tusks. Prehistoric walrus tusk is legal to own and sell still today in Alaska. They then would become one of the most sought-after gifts in Nome. Rudolph the Red Nose Reindeer Nome ornaments were comparable to the Cabbage Patch Dolls in the eighties in the lower forty-eight. All those many years prior, Heather crafting homemade Christmas ornaments when the Smiths had little to no money, all became a full circle event in Nome, Alaska, years later. Those useless vanities were not possible when she was a young child. When Heather wasn't making ornaments and filling orders, she chopped endless amounts of wood. This was an ongoing and never-ending task in Alaska, as common and routine as doing the dishes or the laundry. Another chore that survival in Alaska depended on. Common knowledge in Alaska was to never run low on firewood, or mother nature would send a bitter and harsh reminder. One cold sleepless night would be all it would take to make an Alaskan never run low on the precious commodity of firewood ever again. The Frenchies had to make some serious cold weather adjustments and now owned Reindeer fur coats, complete with mini walrus tusk shape buttons. Pee paths had to be shoveled so they were able to go to the bathroom outside in what seemed like a year-round snow globe that was constantly shaken. On really bad storm days, they would go on emergency pee pads that she kept on hand for blizzards. Most days, they could be found relaxing before a toasty fire, living their best life in sweaters with a moose design on them. Frenchies trying to flourish in Nome, Alaska, was like a fish trying to live out of water. Regardless they adjusted, well, not their attitudes, but their weather acceptance. Heather ensured they were always comfortable; they were beyond spoiled. Brutus and Blue were gaining winter weight along with the rest of Alaska and were hibernating just like the brown bears, in their dens, sound asleep. They both were beginning to look like potbellied pigs wearing little fur coats. Acclamation and changes are never easy, not even for a Frenchie. Like college students that gain the Freshman fifteen, the Frenchies fifteen became a thing.

CHAPTER 7

Asher, Cruz, and Grayson had made the executive decision that they would try out their sea legs and join Dean and Heather on their Alaskan journey to the great unknown. The three of them took on new positions aboard a commercial factory Trawler Vessel working for the United States Seafood Industry. They worked rotating schedules in negative thirty-degree temps most days, processing the fish aboard the vessels. They all spent their days sorting different species, identifying, processing, loading, and packing the fish for the United States Seafood industry. A very tough job, with grueling long wet days and miserable hours at times. Asher, Cruz, and Grayson were always up for a challenge, and hard work never scared them. They enjoyed all their journeys, seeking opportunities to see the world and experience all that it had to offer. Working on a Trawler Vessel for the United States

Seafoods industry was an outrageous experience they certainly would never forget. For it would be an imprint on their work ethics and teach them to appreciate any seafood, they would consume for the rest of their lives. People don't realize the work and the sacrifices others make to plant food on the communities' tables and in their bellies. Most people's comprehension of goods in grocery stores and restaurants stops at the checkout line. They never think about where it originated and all the extreme manpower in subzero temps it took to deliver those goods. These industries pay a decent wage, but the rigid conditions for which these hardworking men and women drudge in day after day are beyond what most people would be able to survive. The Bering Sea offers no sympathy and no relief for the needs of mankind. The saltwater soaks the fishers' bodies to the bone-chilling core, smoothing them out like rocks in a constantly flowing river. They must be resilient, robust, and hardy in order to regale in their fishing landings. Courage is not the absence of fear; rather, it is facing it head-on. Bravery happens when a person is afraid and continues to conquer those fears. Asher, Cruz, and

Grayson had become masteries of their fears. Fear has two meanings in this crazy ride called life. Forget Everything And Run, or Face Everything And Rise.

CHAPTER 8

D ean remained extremely busy and was thriving in his
new Fish and Wildlife career in Alaska. He collected
samples and reported weather patterns and spawning
percentages to Oregon headquarters. While alone along the
Nome River late one fall afternoon, he encountered a
deadly presence unintentionally. He wasn't the only one
trying to figure out the reason for the low levels of the
Chinook Salmon spawn. He smelled something peculiar as
he was making some documentation about the river bank
levels and flow rates. Grizzly Bears will announce
themselves with their strong putrid smell before a sound
can even be heard. It's a musky and fishy smell in the fall
as they prepare themselves for hibernation, consuming
hundreds of pounds of salmon. Dean slowly looks up,
knowing not to make any sudden moves. About thirty
yards down the bank of the Nome River, he sees a nine-

hundred-pound male Grizzly staring back at him with ill intent. Dean can see his ears are back and is beginning to pop his massive bone-crunching jaws. Grizzlies are very territorial, but each bear has its own tolerance and comfort zone. This made the brown bears very unpredictable and threatening. The first sign of aggression is when a Grizzly begins to sway its head and its massive brown hump back and forth. It will pop its jaw and start crackling its massive teeth. The bear will lay its ears back as it continues to snort and release terrifying huffing noises. The Nome River was a popular fishing stretch that would be shared by humans and bears alike. The Alaskan Peninsula Brown Bear was the top of the food chain. The humans were in the same category as the salmon in the Nome River. Although the brown bears are generally solitary species, this time of year produced high levels of concentration of Grizzlies along the Alaskan Rivers. All with the same ending goal of bulking up their fat storage, to take them through to the impending spring while they hibernate for one hundred and fifty-two plus days. Dean had encountered several brown bears in his daily journeys, but this one was much larger and extremely aggressive. Dean figured he must be in this Grizzlies preferred fishing spot. They are highly intelligent and have excellent memories. Dean knowing there was no outrunning a Grizzly Bear who could run fifty miles per hour, remained completely still. Grizzlies are North America's most intelligent nonhuman species, having an IQ around that of a three-year-old human. They have been known to show abilities of counting, using tools, and solving problems like humans. They are very emotionally complex and seem to display this when bothered or frustrated. Dean could tell that this beautiful, majestic, yet deadly creature was contemplating a strategy to return to his well-remembered fishing hole that Dean was hovering over. Planning and thinking through situations was a brown bear's cup of tea in Alaska. Dean decided to try to make the bear understand that he was leaving and didn't mean to intrude on his personal space. Dean put his hands in the air and spoke sternly but intently, trying not to show fear or display any sort of aggression. He explained to the bear that he was just trying to help him with his food sources and wasn't there to tussle with him.

The Grizzly took three steps towards Dean, now stomping his right paw, sinking it into the river banks mud as a warning signal. Dean wholeheartedly took that warning and slowly began to back away from the bank of the river. The Bear didn't care for Dean moving an inch and began to snout louder and curl its black lips in threatening motions. Dean was armed with a forty-five seventy on his chest, the gun that could take down a Grizzly if it was a good shot. This was a last resort for Dean, as he respected the grandness of this beautiful creature. He recognized he was the intruder in this situation, not the brown bear. After the second charge, Dean removed the pistol from his chest, remaining calm and trying to diffuse the bear. Dean took one step at a time backward, not taking his eyes off the Grizzly. Another younger brown bear, little in stature, had approached the bank on the other side of the river, drawing attention to itself. The massive male Grizzly then sees Dean now yards away from his precious gold mine of salmon, relaxed enough for Dean to completely remove himself from harm's way. Now feeling as though he just spent one of his nine lives, Dean was allowed to live to tell

Heather the story. A gift from the Grizzly that made no promises for the next encounter. The Inuit Eskimos worshipped Polar Bears and Brown Bears alike. They believed that the bears would choose which hunters deserved success. Legend says that if the hunters treated the bears properly, the bear would share the news with other bears. They then would be willing to be killed by the Eskimos as well. The Brown Bear is sacred and revered in many cultures. Respect for the most intelligent non-human in North America is known and granted by many worldwide, only rightfully so.

CHAPTER 9

Snow is very common not only during the winter months but also during the summer months on the Bering Sea. The water is a frigid thirty-four degrees on average, year-round, and the sea fog engulfs Nome several days throughout the year. Sea fog appears when warm moist air flows over relatively colder water temps. Waves can exceed forty feet among the treacherous tidal currents, creating a spooky, dark, and gloomy view out of the Summers' cabin windows with the vast views. This sudden onset of coastal fog would make Heather nervous for her sea-baring sons. The Sea Fog was known for causing disorientation and dramatically reduced visibility causing fishermen to become lost at sea. The Fishing Industry would pause for long periods of time, which would cause disrupted productivity for the Trawlers due to the fog. Heather didn't mind; although dangerous and horrifying, these weather patterns grounded her sons from their Bering Sea adventures. Allowing them much-needed downtime with Heather, Dean, and the Frenchies on the mainland. Many nights the Summers would find themselves enjoying one of Earth's greatest and most stunning shows in the sky. The Aurora Borealis, otherwise known as the Northern Lights, would illuminate Nome with its spectacular rays of purple and green.

The lights would dance among themselves as if they were celebrating after a long dark time period. The Inuit have a long-standing legend about the Aurora Borealis; they believe that the dancing lights represent the souls of the dead. The Northern Lights are rich with spiritual traditions about their long-lost departed loved ones. The Inuit call the Aurora the Aksarnirq. Venturing around a mile or two outside the city of Nome, behold some of the most spectacular sights of the Northern Lights in the world. The rich deep purple shades and bright tints of green lights shroud themselves and entwine as a glorious display of dancing miracles. The peak season for such glorious shows of the lights is between August and April.

It's a nice reprieve for the community of Nome, with what seems to be a never-ending midnight with cold dark nights that last forever. The latitude of Nome is sixty-four point-five north, which makes it two degrees south of the arctic circle. This location puts the city of Nome in the perfect placement for the Aurora Borealis to show off night after night. Spending time with the Northern Lights gives the Inuit people a chance to reflect on past memories with their loved ones, who have moved on to dance in the skies in all their glory. Most cultures have their own myths and legends about the Northern Lights, but all lead to the same conclusion about its divine and celestial displays on Earth. For the Summers, Heather in particular, it was a solid reminder about the beauty in a life lived and love that would always remain in the people's souls worldwide. As the Northern lights would Shine brighter in the deep darkness, so did Heather and her three Shining sons. Darkness brings out a brightness that cannot be seen until the darkness has set in deep. Guardian Angels are a lot like the Aurora when it comes to Shining the brightest when it is the darkest. As the lights dance among themselves in worldly celebrations, the seasons of people's lives storm on. The memories that would return to the Summers were not all peaceful celebrations but reminders of their tasks and assignments that would hold them to their duties on Earth. Heather's duty was not Smitty the Fallen Angel but another yet to be discovered. Heather was meant to find Dean, her husband, the Seer. Who would then have a task of his own, which was Smitty? Seers are not Guardians; they are people on this planet that have the capability of opening their third eye. Opening this third eye gives them crystal ball-like divine visions of the future. This can be a wonderful gift and feel like a horrid curse all at the same time. Knowing the impending outcomes for Seers and their loved ones is a soul sucker. It can leave Seers with a feeling of no hope for the negative visions that appear to them. While at the same time, it can give them nothing but hope for their visions' overly divine positive outcomes. It's completely a Yin and Yang kind of existence for Seers. Again, like most things in life, you can't have one without the other.

Where there is a positive, there will always be a negative.

CHAPTER 10

Now living in Fargo, North Dakota, Penelope found herself on a spiritual journey. She was taking it one day at a time. For this would be the rest of her life's purpose. To heal herself and learn to live without evil around her. In most cases, adjusting outside the realms of abuse is painstaking and unfamiliar. Newly gained freedom after abuse creates a lot of self-doubt and self-harming thoughts. Regret is one of the toughest emotions to overcome. Hindsight is said to be twenty-twenty and a cruel and relentless jerk. Hindsight only lets the person understand their past experiences and tragic situations after the fact. Almost as if it is laughing and saying, "I told you so," once hindsight knows it's too late. It's a tough lesson to bare for most abuse survivors. Many only ask themselves why people stay in abusive situations rather than what they should be asking, which is, why are people abusing others? The questions always seem to fall on the survivors instead of falling in their rightful place with the abusers. Survivors must learn not to make themselves victims and products of their abuse and abusers. Constantly playing the victim makes the abuser more in control and can blueprint the abuse in a maleficent design. It gives a false sense of power to the evil. Fallen Angels eat this up like it's their last dinner. That was Penelope's life for decades, and she now had to be a survivor instead of a victim. Never having been alone in her life and suffering from codependency habits made for a lonely time in Fargo. She spent her days working at a local western shop selling clothing, boots, and hats. She buried herself in her workload most days to dull the pain of missing the dangerous comfort zones she was accustomed to all those years. Although she didn't miss the evil in her life, she felt misplaced and omitted. Lacking all comfort zones made her a bit absent in her life. Heather would call from Nome, Alaska, and check in with Penelope most weeks; hearing the progress of her journey over the phone gave Heather a peaceful easy feeling. Heather was Penelope's Guardian

Angel and had guided her to her divine journey in Nebraska. Part of that process was removing Smitty, her husband, the Fallen Angel, from Penelope's spiritual surroundings. Dean taking that undertaking upon himself with Violet's Archangel Blade, left Heather with a divine assignment still ahead of her. Asher, Cruz, and Greyson, Heather's celestial soldiers, also still had a divine mission to complete.

CHAPTER 11

Heather cherished all her memories with Violet, her Archangel Grandmother, and was so blessed in knowing that Violet had Heather's back even though she no longer walked this Earth. Violet had placed that Archangel Blade in Dean's hands well before he was actually to hold the blade in his Seeing visions and perform the duty he knew he had to perform. While watching the dancing Northern Lights, she smiled during one of the Summer nightly strolls outside of Nome. Heather would think of her Grandmother, Violet the Archangel. Violet, who loved to dance and would only marry a man who could dance her into a heavenly abyss, was dancing gloriously in the sky above her. With her gold-gilded gray wings, Violet had earned her glory and crowns in heaven. She now could dance with joy, holding her two babies that had passed after birth. Violet could twirl her baby girl and a baby boy around while the white baptismal gowns they were buried in would flow in the wind with such grace and pureness. After decades of yearning for their smell, she could now kiss and hug them. The last thing Violet did before laying her two babies to rest was lean down and smell the tops of their heads. Mothers always know their baby's smell and never forget it. Losing one child is something a mother's heart never can recover from, so losing two was a pain beyond comprehension. Being an Archangel, Violet felt this loss more deeply and severely than a normal person would. Archangels and Guardian Angels feel grief, agony, and the throbbing discomforts of loss in a heightened level down to their souls. Their unconditional love runs deeper than humanly possible. It stings deep with a smarting pain and an aching that consumes them. Violet's depression was not the focus of her Demon battle with her brother Bert, who sexually abused her as a child. It was for the loss of her beloved newborns after two full-term pregnancies and having to leave the hospital without her newborn baby, not once, but twice. Violet knew they were in good hands in the Celestial

Kingdom but couldn't help her yearning for her babies. Their place was always meant to be in the divine kingdom, and Violet had to live her life on Earth without them until she returned. Not only did Heather have a sister she had never met and never walked among them, but Penelope did as well. She had a sister and a brother whom she had never met, and her mother, Violet, was now holding them both. Penelope could picture this, and it always made her feel so happy and relieved for her mother, Violet, who could now store the sorrow away forever.

CHAPTER 12

Some memories would always stand out to Heather as she, too, would reflect in the dancing lights of the Aurora Borealis. One that always seemed to want to return time and time again was Violet's passion for feeding all the birds and squirrels in her Lilac filled backyard. Nothing ever went to waste with Violet. The critters that lived in her backyard would always benefit from Violet's table scraps, as she would call them. Her back steps would sometimes look like a scene out of the movie Snow White. Birds, rabbits, and gray squirrels would surround the plates of scraps, all eating together. Violet had one critter she didn't care for, and she made it very known.

The red squirrels would be Violet's not-so-favorite for the better part of her life. Red squirrels are known to be unsociable, highly territorial, and very aggressive. They are bullies to their own kind and the beautiful bushy-tailed gray squirrels. Violet would call them chatterbox bullies. When they would come around for a scrap or two, all the other critters would scatter and hide. Violet would watch this knowing that the red chatterboxes were nasty to everything else around it. Reds didn't like the beautiful gray and would react in a jealous manner. The chatterboxes are always up for a fight and always make waves in what would otherwise be a very serene part of nature. Violet would tell Heather about people that were also chatterboxes and would make others scatter just as the red squirrel would. These people are usually the takers among givers. Where there are peacemakers, there will always be people causing conflict. It's really a sad and disheartening part of life, Violet would say, as she would point out that it existed in humanity and in nature. In Mythology, the red squirrel is the one who runs up and down the trees with messages spreading gossip and rumors. Although the reds are mean and selfish, they most certainly can hold their own. They don't hibernate in the winter but instead live off the food they have gathered and buried in up to a foot of snow. They are extremely resilient and tough. People and nature are products of their environment. The red squirrel must be aggressive in order to survive the long, harsh winters. It doesn't go south or hibernate like the other critters; it knows its impending doom if it doesn't fight for its right to survive. Also, gray squirrels carry a disease called Para poxvirus. This disease does not appear to affect the gray squirrel's health at all but oftentimes will kill the red squirrels. Due to the reds knowing this about the grays, the reds will bite off the gray's testes in a territorial battle. Everything and everyone have some sort of contribution to give to life as we know it. The universe creates itself out of primary chaos and material energy. Yin symbolizes the earth, the female, darkness, and passivity. Yang is heaven, the male, light, and activity. Summer and winter, night and day, retreating and advancing, the weak and the strong are all part of the universe's cycles of life.

CHAPTER 13

Nome, Alaska, can be a very peaceful yet extremely lonely place on this planet. It's filled with long days of darkness, endless nights of freezing double-digit below zero temps, and entirely isolated. This gives the people of Nome more time to reflect and dwell on past regrets and heartbreaking memories that seem to consume them like the fog that rolls off the sea. The dreary, damp weather always seems to aid in their sadness. The suicide rate is the highest in Nome compared to other surrounding regions of Alaska. Another Nome mystery lies deep in its darkest glacier depths. In town, there were not a ton of stores and shops, so the choices were minimal. The Eagle's Landing Grocery was a hot spot in town for all the locals. The store owner was a mysterious individual who always seemed to dislike everyone and everything around him. He was a sad soul, lost in a world of isolation. The deep-set wrinkles on his grimacing face showed signs of a long, hard life. His face looked leathery and weather-beaten from years of Alaskan winters. He was known by the locals as the once-five-time champion of the Iditarod Dog Sled Race several decades previous. His dog sled breeding line of malamutes was world-renowned, and everyone knew of him and his award-winning sled dogs. His name was Nanook. The name Nanook stands for Polar Bear in the Inuit culture. Inuit tribes take great care with picking babies' names. They usually are named after elders, hunters, and exceptional people with great accomplishments. They believe that a name carries a great weight, and they have strong beliefs around how their babies' names are chosen. This can take weeks for them to decide once the baby is born, and they make this decision with hours of thought put into the name. Nanook's father was a great Polar Bear hunter. He was named after him. His stories and tales will continue for generations to come. Nanook's father was named Hanta. The name Hanta in the Inuit culture means hunter. Hanta was one of the greatest Polar Bear hunters in the tribe in his day. He was known to be able to take on the almost impossible challenge of battling Polar Bears with only a handmade spear and his long-standing courage. This was one of the necessary means of the tribe's survival during the harshest winter climates on the planet. They would use every single part of the bear's meat, fur, and claws. Inuit's left no waste of the animal they would bless after hunting. While hunting, they would pay deep respect to the spirit of the animal. If they did not pay this respect to the animal that they were hunting, the belief is that the animal would then appear to them as a Demon. After an Inuit hunt, they would pray for the spirits of the harvested animals. It was necessary to appease these spirits for a successful hunting and fishing season in the years to come. They also feared the spirits taking revenge on the community if they were not respected and thanked properly. After the animal's death, the Inuit belief is that if it was treated with the utmost respect, the animal was reborn. The animal is believed to allow itself to be hunted again in its next incarnation. Although many Inuit today follow Christianity, their traditional Inuit spirituality is animism and shamanism. This is the practice of which spiritual healers mediate with spirits. Nanook came from a long line of respected hunters and elders. Therefore he, too, was a respected member of the Inuit community. Like his father before him, he also supplied a much-needed substance to the Inuit community. His grocery store was a lifeline for Nome's isolated and locked-tight town. Without his store, life would be near impossible for the town and its population to flourish year-round. The Summer's, just like all the other community members, shopped at Eagle's Landing. When Heather and her family would enter the store, Nanook could see them and their shine. The Summers knew he could see them as four people who Shined. For the look on his weathered, beaten face told them without any actual dialog being spoken. Nanook practiced shamanism and was a highly respected Shaman of his tribe, and he could see the Shine. Inuit Shamans are known to be religious leaders, tradesmen, healers, and characters holding mysterious, powerful, and sometimes superhuman strength. Heather and Nanooks eyes would meet, speaking a universal language to each other. They both believed in Demons and evil among them. Nanook was a healer who could see the Shine.

CHAPTER 14

Heather found comfort whenever she shopped in town at the Eagle's Landing Grocery. Nanook was a feeling of home and pureness among all the isolation in Nome. Although he never smiled or showed any sign of that through his actions, Heather knew. She knew who he was, and he knew who she was. It wasn't a complex understanding; Rather, it was a mutual respect. Nanook had people misunderstand him just as Heather did. Nanook was looked upon as a great healer, but people also feared the unknown. They feared his abilities, his powers, and his mysterious ways of healing. Most of the time, no known scientific explanation could be found of his healing outcomes and results. Just as people pray for Angels and Healers, they never truly want to see them with their own eyes. Most of the time, it's spiritually unexplainable and frightening for the average person. They know that some things just can't be unseen, and their lives will forever be changed. Their comforts would be questioned, and their beliefs would be officially confirmed. Confirmation of beliefs is something people struggle with, maybe they were wrong about something, or maybe they were completely right. Both are very scary concepts to most humans on this Earth. Where does that leave a person once they have that kind of knowledge, completely lost within what they always thought was the truth or what they thought were always lies, now presented as the absolute truth. The only place they are left is in a complex mind-blowing stage and a rigid feeling of not being in control. Both things humans strive for, truth they don't really want to know and complete control, which they never will truly obtain. Just when people think they have all the answers and the blue prints to life, life proves to them they absolutely do not. Life seems to have a good chuckle about what humans think they know and what humans think they can control. This is Fate. The Summers were meant to move to Nome, Alaska, and Heather was meant to cross paths with Nanook, the Inuit Shaman. Heather found herself at the

Eagle's Landing with Nanook more and more as the days in Alaska went by. There was just something about being in his presence that gave her a sense of peace and tranquility. Nanook also enjoyed seeing Heather's face even though he never expressed it or led her to believe otherwise. There was a sense of belonging and familiarness about Heather that Nanook longed for. Being in a tribe doesn't always cure feelings of complete loneliness; ironic as that seems, it's the sad truth. Nanook was the healer of his tribe; therefore, they only came to him with health issues, grief, and sadness most days. That leaves a Shaman with not only his demons but with the entire tribe's as well. Heather knew he would be a hard egg to crack, but she was determined to break through. The day had finally arrived when she saw how deep his pain had run. In an already isolated part of the world, his heart was stranded on an island, starved for food and shelter. Heather was picking up the usual milk, eggs, and bread when she felt a presence. She turned around to find Nanook standing behind her with no expression on his face, but he was holding his hand out as if he was trying to hand her something. Heather reached out her hand, and he placed an ivory-carved baby seal necklace in her hand. This carving was the most beautiful thing she had ever seen. Nanook began to tell her how he carves animals and jewelry out of walrus ivory as a hobby in his spare time and on long winter nights. In the Inuit culture seals symbolize innocence. Therefore, the Inuit translations in the bible follow the tribal people. The Inuit tribe replace the word "Lamb" in the Bible with the word "Seal." Although Nanook's pieces could easily be museum pieces on display, the Inuit people do not consider their carvings art. Matter of fact, there is no word for art in the Inuit language. The tribe calls such carvings and sculptures sananguagait, which means objects that are made or small replicas of real articles. They are sometimes referred to as trade sculptures. Sedna is said to be the sea goddess for the Inuit people. She is said to hold the sea animals entangled in her hair. It is said she only releases them when she is appeased by offerings, songs, or a visit from an Angakok, otherwise known as a Shaman. This was Nanook's way of reassuring Heather about all her assumptions about him and that she had been correct.

Heather was speechless, she had rehearsed in her mind a thousand times what she would say to Nanook when the moment presented itself, yet she couldn't speak. Nanook nodded and turned around, leaving Heather holding a piece of art like no other. She tied the reindeer leather that the baby seal was dangling from around her neck and stood there reflecting in the moment. Heather finished shopping and proceeded to the front of the store to pay for her grocery items and check out. Nanook was waiting for her behind the register as if he knew he was going to finally speak with Heather but seemed extremely uncomfortable about it. Heather walked closer to the register and realized that although she had already seen him hundreds of times in the store and around town, she had never truly seen him until that moment.

CHAPTER 15

Instead of the crabby wrinkled weary face, she seemed to have witnessed many times before, this time; she was noticing something else. She saw decades of unexplainable knowledge; every weathered wrinkle told its own story. Years of endless healing and unimaginable heartbreak. The kind that Heather and her sons carried for all the ones who didn't Shine and for all who were guarded by them. The kind of pain and compassion for others that only Guardian Angels and Shaman can hold deep in their souls. Average mankind could never handle such distress, knowledge, and torment, for it would destroy them to their deepest depths. Although Heather and Nanook seemed to be from completely different worlds, they were really one and the same. Wandering through the world alone, misunderstood, and having people depend on them endlessly. Whether those people realize it or not doesn't change the endless expectations people have toward a Guardian Angel or Shaman. Nanook wasn't a crabby old Inuit man; he was a Guardian Angel among his people, with years of experiences and stories that he wore on his face like a worn-out road map. The wrinkles presented themselves as ravines and ridges through his life. The harder his heart and soul had to work, the deeper the wrinkles they caused. The shallow wrinkles represented themselves as assignments not yet completed, with a "To-be-continued" look to them. The deep onset crow's feet on either side of his dark eyes were his journeys in flight. They were the countless miracles he had witnessed throughout decades of his practice. Although his eyes were the darkest Heather had ever seen, they looked as though she could see right through them. As she approached the counter, she never took her eyes off his. Heather began to thank Nanook for the stunning ivory-carved baby seal necklace when he interrupted her, saying only the words "Not necessary" with a tiny bit of a smile. The wrinkles that drug his smile down with such force were removed for only a second. Heather knew what the baby seal meant to the Inuit people and how the word "Lamb" in the Bible was changed to "Seal" by the Inuit. This was also Nanooks way of telling Heather he knew that she Shined and that she was sent to this world just as he was. Not another word was spoken as Nanook rang up all the groceries. Heather gathered up her brown paper bags and began to leave the store, pushing the door open with her back as her arms were full. She stopped for a second and looked back at Nanook; he was now standing in front of the counter in all his glory with a ginormous mask covering his entire face. It had massive reindeer antlers presenting themselves from the very top. She could see the mask was carved out of walrus ivory and had eagle feathers protruding all around it. The mask was smiling with sharp white ivory teeth carved inside the smile with brightly painted colors. A round, sharp-looking object made of driftwood was protruding outwards from the mask's base. The mask had two sets of nostrils, one on top of the other, with jet-black eyes set wider than normal on either side of the mask. On his hands were two sets of claws. They were ivory pieces carved with five two-foot-long carvings representing fingers. Inuit Shamans covering their heads and hands was the traditional means of safeguarding themselves from evil and spiritual forces. His reindeer fur parka was trimmed with beautiful reindeer leather fringe. On the chest of the parka, two white hand prints were sown into the fur with white rabbit fur. Below the handprints were three white fox fur circles with a sun beam-like design; these held three pieces of beautiful bright red beads dangling from three pieces of reindeer fringe. On the shoulders of the parka, two seal fur arrows were pointing at each other on each shoulder. Above the two white fur handprints was an Inuit figure of a person highlighted in beaver fur. The parka went past Nanook's knees and joined a pair of reindeer fur boots trimmed with otter and calfskin. Heather knew Nanook was showing her "His" shine. This was the ritualistic mask, parka, and gloves that an Inuit Medicine Man would wear to exorcise evil spirits and "Work to bear the devil," as an Inuit Shaman would say. Heather stood there halfway between the store's doorway, in complete awe of what was being presented to her by Nanook, the Inuit Medicine Man. Nanook was now part of Heather's army as he stood before her with his battle armor on and ready to go to battle with Heather and her family. The Summers were destined to move to Nome, Alaska, and discovering Nanook the Shaman was nothing short of divine fate.

CHAPTER 16

Penelope was planning on spending Christmas in Alaska with the Summers. She had been handling her newfound freedom in North Dakota with grace, and Heather thought it was time for a visit. Penelope also wanted Heather to invite Cassie to Alaska for Christmas, so Heather reached out, and Cassie accepted. Cassie was still single as far as Heather knew, so she didn't extend an invite to a plus-one for Cassie. Penelope and Cassie had to fly into Anchorage first and then take a smaller plane into Nome. Since there is no road system in or out of Nome, that is the only option. The Summers were joyful to have family visiting them in their new home in Alaska but also weary since they hadn't seen either since the incident in Nebraska with Smitty the Fallen Angel. Cassie was unaware of the real reason for Smitty's sudden disappearance from Nebraska. Penelope always planned on telling Cassie the honest truth about everything but always felt it wasn't a good time. When is it ever a good time to tell someone that their father was a malevolent Fallen Angel set out for destruction and ruin? There is no right time or place for that kind of conversation piece, and certainly not over the phone. Penelope thought maybe she could have Heather help her tell Cassie the truth in Alaska over Christmas. Since some time had passed, Penelope thought maybe Cassie wouldn't take it so hard. Heather, unaware of Penelope's plans, had a feeling that things would not go as planned. It rarely did with Penelope; she was a broken person with broken ways of doing things. To no fault of her own, it was as if she couldn't help herself and didn't know any better. Regardless, the Summers prepared the cabin for guests with extra quilts and chopped extra firewood for the cold nights. Penelope had adjusted to the cold nights living in North Dakota, but Cassie, having moved to California, would certainly not be. Cassie was chasing acting dreams on the west coast and still living her life to the fullest. Although she was getting older and should soon settle down, that was not her style. Nothing was going to stop her goals and dreams of becoming a somebody someday. The three boys were back off the trawler boats for the holiday, and Dean was off on vacation, so everyone would be around. Dean once again seemed extra quiet while the preparations for their guests were being made. Heather and the three boys just assumed Penelope and Cassie's visit was bringing back unwanted memories of what Dean was forced to do in Nebraska. Smitty would forever remain land locked in all their brains, but for Dean, it would always remain very dark. Dark as night. Heather never told the boys or Dean about Nanook and what went on that day in the Eagle's Landing. She only showed Dean and the boys the ivory baby seal necklace Nanook gave Heather that day. Dean smiled as if he already knew the story behind this generous offering. The three boys knew what the seal represented to the Inuit people. They all nodded in unison as if they also were already aware of the significance behind the gift from Nanook. Christmas was a few short weeks away, and with guests coming, the Summers were decorating and getting ready. The Summers all went to the forest and cut down the most beautiful Christmas Tree to decorate and store the gifts under. The tree was a nine-foot-tall Mountain Hemlock, filling the cabin with the most wonderful pine smell. It was nothing short of Christmas paradise in the Summer's Alaskan cabin. The fire roaring and tree smell made it a picture-perfect place to spend Christmas. Heather had handmade all the gifts. She had made both her mother and her sister reindeer gloves lined with arctic fox fur on the cuffs. The insides of the gloves were the softest beaver fur imaginable, and she was sure they would use them during their visit to the bitter Alaskan tundra. She also made them both matching white Arctic fox hats. They looked like the hats Russian designers would make for the runways. The Mountain Hemlock tree displayed a combination of rustic animal ornaments and glass-blown ornaments, all made by the Inuit locals of Nome. The Frenchies had beaver coats with hoods that Heather had made for extreme cold days with matching beaver booties for their paws. With Christmas music playing in the background, the cozy cabin looked, smelled, and sounded like a scene from a Norman Rockwell painting. Heather wanted to give her family a Christmas to remember; little did she know it would be, but not for the reasons she had assumed. The weather was supposed to let up just in time for Penelope and Cassie to arrive without delay. They were to arrive the week before Christmas and stay through the new year. The Summer's made sure to stock up with plenty of food with extra people expected to be in the cabin. The unpredictable storms that quickly came off the Bering Sea made emergency food essential. Heather handmade Nanook a Christmas ornament as his gift. It was Nanook in his Shaman Ritual mask and gloves. It was an exact replica of his parka and boots down to the last detail, with the white hands on the chest and fringe. Heather had seen him display it to her only once. Regardless, it was photocopied into her brain, and she could never unsee it. The mask was identical to what she had seen with the teeth, bright colors, and even the feathers. The only difference was that the feathers could not be Eagle feathers on Heather's ornament. Inuit people can only gift Eagle feathers to other Inuit, never to non-Inuit people. They are able to pass them down from generation to generation, but only among the Inuit tribal people. Heather used dyed turkey feathers, which resemble Eagle feathers the most. The Summers arrived at Nanook's grocery store to pick up the remaining items for the next few weeks. Nanook was busy stocking the shelves when he felt a presence; he turned around to find Heather standing there with her hand out, handing him something. He took the Shaman ornament from Heather's hand and stared at it silently for a moment. He then looked up to see Heather smiling with the brightest yellow sparkling glow around her he had seen since their paths first crossed. He also saw her glorious silver-tipped wings showing off to him in all their glory. Nanook's eyes followed the wings all the way to the ceiling of the store as they were almost touching the very top. He then looked back at Heather, and as their eyes met once again, he allowed his face to turn what seemed like a permanent frown upside down. Even though he didn't have the whitest or the best teeth, Heather saw the most beautiful smile she had ever seen. The fact that he could smile through all the pain trapped inside his soul was a miracle. Heather was seeing him, and he was seeing her.

Just then, Dean came around the corner and smiled an "It's about time" smile. He said to the both of them, standing there in all their shine, "Glad you two finally met." Laughing and shaking his head, he went on with his grocery list. Dean left Heather and Nanook to embrace in the most special of all divine hugs between two Angels from what seemed like worlds apart, yet one and the same.

CHAPTER 17

Penelope was the first to arrive for the holidays in the little locked-up sleepy town of Nome. The Summers were all there to greet her at that little airport, which was more like a landing for a puddle jumper than a jet. Heather saw her and knew North Dakota had treated her well and helped her heal and learn how to be alone in peace rather than surrounded by chaos. A comfort zone that would take Penelope time to adjust within. She was still wearing the Holy Water that Heather had gifted her that sobering day in the Nebraska garden. As Heather watched her step down the plane's stairs, she noticed that Penelope looked healthy but had also aged some. The wrinkles around her eyes could tell folks stories for hours. Most people wouldn't believe most of the tales she could tell them, but she didn't need to tell her side of the story. For everyone would know her truth and torment someday, if not in this world, certainly in the next. Asher, Cruz, and Grayson went to embrace her and welcome their grandmother to Nome, Alaska. Heather and Dean stayed back, giving them their time alone with her. Her hugs seemed different to the boys this time. Almost as if they were tighter and stronger than before. Even her grandson's hugs had more confidence than they had ever demonstrated to their grandmother, as if cherishing it for the last time. As Heather and Dean approached the three boys giving her a bear hug, her eyes met with Penelope's. Unspoken words were said in that moment. Many years of gratitude and appreciation poured out of Penelope's eyes like a bright blue waterfall. Heather could also see the long-standing pain that would forever remain in her mother's eyes and her soul. Some things in life just can't be unseen and tattoo themselves on people's souls as a reminder of their journeys. Tattoos of the past are meant to stay as lessons, not punishments. Reflections of how far a person has come and the painful past that shaped them into who they were always meant to be in life. It is not anyone's place to ask why, for the questions will soon be answered. Heather embraced Penelope with a softer and more exhausted tightness. Heather was beyond drained from her Guardian Angel assignment with Penelope. It was a lifelong assignment for Heather that had taken every ounce of divine energy she had throughout her long life with Penelope and Smitty. It involved abuse and mistreatment on the highest levels, feelings not even Angels can avoid or overlook. As a matter of fact, Angels feel it deeper than the average person, and it sticks to their hearts and souls like superglue. Watching humans destroy others, and themselves is a complete torment to a Guardian Angel. It goes against everything they are assigned to believe in and destined to strive for. Penelope embraced Dean with a tough love hug. Even though she knew Dean did what had to be done, a little piece of Penelope would always yearn for that unhealthy comfort zone named Smitty. She would never admit this to anyone, but no less it existed within her. Dean was tolerable with this, he knew he had done what was best for his family, and that was all that mattered. Being reasonable was not a trait an abused person could develop overnight, even if they know right from wrong. Cassie wasn't coming in till the next day, so the Summers had time with Penelope alone. Nothing was said about Smitty, for it was in the past and needed to remain there. The past was meant to remain in the past so the future could take its place. Heather knew that talking about Smitty with Penelope would only slow down the progression of her spiritual journey. The journey that Heather was assigned to guide Penelope towards. On the other hand, Penelope planned to confess the truth to Cassie during the visit but didn't discuss this with Heather.

CHAPTER 18

Dean was very quiet during dinner that first night that Penelope was at the cabin. This always meant he was having a vision. Being a Seer, he couldn't control when the visions would appear or how. A Seer is a person that has supernatural insight and can sometimes see what the future holds. He always described it to Heather and the three boys as visions were warning signs when something would soon occur. The exact timing of this was never revealed in the visions; Dean would just know when it was time. Heather knew better than to try to get Dean to open up about the visions; he would only do so on his terms. Most of the time, those terms were "Never"; for the sake of his family's feelings or maybe his own. Either way, the visions were his, and him to do with what he thought was right. Dean never had good timing with anything in life, and his visions were no different. Maybe the visions caused these poor calculations in his life, and maybe not. Maybe Dean orchestrated them exactly how and when he felt he should. Heather always felt that he had more control over them than he led on, but only time would tell. Everyone has their Demons, and this was Deans. He had chosen to leave the family that raised him by the wayside due to the visions and outcomes he had foreseen. Heather and the boys never passed judgment and trusted in Dean that he knew what was best for himself and his future. Heather always felt in her heart that Dean had been physically abused as a child, and that was where his reasons and demons remained. He once opened up to Asher, Cruz, and Grayson about being beaten many times as a young child with belts. Dean was an unusual child with a lot of social issues because of the visions he would have at such a young age. Again, people don't like things they don't understand, things that confuse them. He told many lies, some for the good of others but mostly as a protection mechanism because he was a scared little boy. He couldn't understand what was happening, so neither could anyone around him. He continued this way of life throughout his entire life. Lie after lie, a habit Dean the Seer would never kick throughout his life. Seers are scared of being "Seen" for who they are, ironically. Judgment of being different and weird was bound to be the only conclusion from others. The boys never questioned Dean's motives about his past; after that time, Dean expressed how he was beaten as a child. Heather and Dean had abuse in common. Although different types of abuse, they all tend to leave the same shape scars, some visible and others not. Dean did show signs of anger and rage, but not very often. Most of the time, he dealt with his demons and visions solely on his own. Heather and the boys could see torment within him but knew there was nothing they could say or do to change anything. He would never be honest or tell them the full truth, so they all knew not to question him. Heather liked to think he did this to protect her and the boys, but deep in her heart, she knew he was doing it for his own protection and self-preservation, not theirs. Being a Seer is like being several people all at once. Seers are passive heart seekers, usually the focus of attention tactically, and exhibit extreme ultimatums. They have their present life, their past situations, and the ability to see some future events. It's a little like living three different lives all at once. The saying that feels like a lifetime ago is an understatement for a Seer. Heather being a Guardian Angel, could see right through Dean but was unable to hold grudges or judgement. Those were Dean's Demons to battle. Heather had plenty of her own walking and talking Demons to deal with.

CHAPTER 19

Heather and Penelope were early risers making all the men pancakes and getting ready to head to the airport to pick up Cassie. Both were excited to see her and hear all about her Cali life and all the cool people she was meeting and greeting. She always had some crazy funny story to tell. Nice change of pace in a much too serious life they all led. Penelope was nervous and cleaned the cabin more than usual, knowing her plans with Cassie. Penelope always cleaned when she was upset or anxious about something, so Heather was aware that Penelope was upset. Heather, not wanting to get into anything with Penelope, just as they are about to get Cassie, lets it go. They all got in the Tahoe and headed to the airport. Penelope was silent the entire drive there. She was staring out the window as if she was in another world and not physically present in Alaska. Heather could see in the rear-view mirror the torment on Penelope's face as they got closer and closer to the airport. The look in Penelope's eyes was a look that was all too familiar to Heather. The look of regret and reckoning. Heather then knew what Penelope was planning and plotting on doing. Heather told Penelope that they were almost there and then said, "Mom, the truth always lies in the eyes of the beholder." Penelope, taken aback by what Heather just said, just stared at Heather with a shocked look on her face. No one in the Tahoe said another word till they arrived at the airport. Dean then says with a stern voice as he opens the truck door, "Be careful who you trust; salt and sugar always seem to look the same." Heather pauses before exiting the truck, knowing that was a warning. They all are waiting for Cassie to exit the plane, but she is taking forever, and everyone seems to be off the plane already when they finally see her round the airplane door. She is dressed in a faux fur leopard print jacket, a black leather mini skirt, and tall brown rockstar-looking boots with buckles, and her hair is now bright red, short, and super curly. Heather and Penelope look at each other, shrug, and start to giggle. Dean is standing much further back when Heather turns to look for him. The boys start heading towards the plane to greet their crazy aunt, Cassie, all laughing and shaking their heads. Dean doesn't move but holds his ground in anticipation. Just as Cassie is about halfway down the plane's stairs, she quickly turns around while giggling up a storm. Heather then stops and watches as Cassie joins a man at the top of the stairs dressed in a very expensive Armani three-piece suit and a bright red tie. She is kissing him on the lips, saying something to him, and he is laughing. His smile is smug and irritating. Asher, Cruz, and Grayson all stop in their tracks and look back at Heather. Heather is standing there frozen as she also sees the handsome, expensively dressed man embracing and kissing Cassie. That is not all that she sees. He was surrounded by a black shadow Shining around him that almost looked like a cape. His hair was as dark as night, and his eyes were the brightest blue. He almost looked like Dracula exiting that plane, but Heather and her boys knew that wasn't a vampire. That was a Demon. Heather held her breath unknowingly as she turned to see Dean nodding his head up and down, letting

Heather know he had seen this "Thing" and this moment coming. Penelope, unable to see the Shine like the rest of them, stands there, surprised Cassie brought a plus one with her. As Heather watches the two of them slowly walk down the stairs, she feels a presence. She looks to the right of her, and off in the distance, she sees him. She sees Nanook standing there in all his Shaman glory. Just as she had seen him that day at the Eagle's Landing Grocery. He is also nodding as the mask and massive reindeer antlers are moving up and down in a slow-motion movement. No one else sees the fully armored Shaman standing there but Heather. As she turns back around, she notices that Asher, Cruz, and Grayson are back by Heather's side in silence, watching Cassie and her sharply dressed beau approach them. Dean remains behind Heather and the three boys with his arms crossed on his chest. Penelope, not knowing what she is approaching, is the first to go to Cassie and what Penelope thinks is a nice-looking gentleman. Heather watches as Penelope hugs Cassie and then hugs the Demon Cassie introduces her to. As the newly unwanted house guest embraces Penelope, his chest touches the Holy

Water necklace hiding under Penelope's sweater, and he yanks himself back quickly. He looks at Heather after he is taken back and felt a very painful burning feeling from the divine Holy Water. He then smiles the evilest wicked of grins bearing his bright white perfect teeth at Heather. He was taunting Heather, Asher, Cruz, and Grayson with his smile. Heather knows he sees her and her three sons Shining bright divinely, and he knows they all see him Shining dark malevolently. All love-struck and excited, Cassie runs over and starts hugging all the boys and Heather. Heather then says to Cassie, "You didn't tell us you were bringing a guest." Cassie replies to Heather with a smile, "Spencer wanted to make it a surprise, isn't he something." Just then, Spencer walks over to Heather, forces a hug on her, and whispers in Heather's ear, "Nice to meet you, Heather; Cassie has told me so much about you, oh, and Smitty says Trick or Treat."

CHAPTER 20

Heather and Dean had always known that the ordeal with Smitty wouldn't ever be completely terminated, and he would somehow and in some way weasel his malevolent way back into their story. Demons always base their endings on having the last laugh. Peace for the Summers was merely an illusion with tiny wisps of happiness. The absence of eternal peace comes with the territory of Guardians and Seers. They puree together like peas and carrots around pot roast. Can't seem to have one without the other for a complete entree. Even though most people don't like peas, let's be honest; they would be missed in some sort of an unwanted yet needed way. Life seems to need its peas; wanted or not, there they always are. There's a reason why there is no ice cream, gum, or candy pea flavored. Heather knew after the sighting at the Eagle's Landing Grocery and at the airport that her army also had a plus one. Nanook was all in his armor and ready to fight evil at a moment's notice. It sure is interesting how two different walks of life can come together when goodness and pureness are the objective. All the different cultures in the world, for the most part all, have the same objectives in this life. Good always outways evil, and love seems to win over hate. Not always, but that is the goal in most situations. Goodness and pure love have more to lose; therefore, their fight means something much more powerful and deeper than evil and hate. Heather and her family had so much more to lose than Spencer ever would, and they had time on their side. With time comes experience, and this wasn't their first rodeo with evil. This one was bold, confident, and had been sent from Hell as a messenger from Smitty, as a way to reach Heather and her family. He was to deliver a message, and Heather had received it from Spencer loud and clear. Spencer was from Cali; that's where Cassie had first been introduced to him. He was a film producer, and Cassie was a yearning young free spirit that thought she could make it on the big screen someday. Little did she know he wasn't interested in her acting abilities. Matter of fact, he laughed at her behind her back, knowing she just didn't have what it took to make it in his world. A small-town innocent Nebraska girl thinking she could play with the big dogs should have stayed on the porch was his real take on her. Regardless, he had been sent to destroy Cassie and her Shining sister Heather. Penelope was no longer concerned for Smitty; his concern now was his ultimate revenge on the Summers. His untimely death was premature and disrupted his chess game. He was caught by surprise with an early checkmate. Smitty didn't like to lose and was being tortured once again in Hell by his master Satan for failing his assignments. Satan was a poor loser and made his followers pay a hefty price. He ultimately blamed all his followers for losing the battle against the heavens and would never allow them to forget it. Torcher is what he had crafted as his masterpiece. Creating some of the worst Demons with the most horrific of intentions to be sent back to earth to deliver evil messages and mayhem from him directly. Payback to the heavens, making them watch humans on Earth being taken over and enslaved by Demons, was how he refueled and flourished evil within. Spencer Doyle was a sophisticated movie producer. He knew how to dress, act and persuaded women into doing just about anything he wanted them to do. The name Doyle translates into "Dark stranger," which was exactly what Spencer was, a dark stranger. He took advantage of his good looks and power every chance he got. Upcoming Hollywood debutantes didn't stand a chance with his utterly captivating smile and unpredictable sexual attraction. The beautiful women wanting to make it on the big screen someday were his prey and were easy pickings for a dark stranger with ill intentions and a goal of ruin. Women who thought they could sleep their way to the top were all one at a time checked off Spencer's list like a to-do list crossed off daily. Cassie was just too perfect; not only could he check her off of his to-do list, but he could also gain access to Heather and her family per Smitty's request. Sometimes life is just too perfectly placed for evil. From the moment Cassie saw his smile, his walk, and how he held her so confidently and strongly, it was game over. She couldn't have seen through Spencer and his evil plans and motives even if she had tried. She was too blinded by love and sexually obsessed, and her Hollywood goals were a top priority. Spencer said all the right things, did all the right things and made her feel what she thought was complete. The sex was indescribable and passionate. Spencer had mastered his art on his prey, and in this area, he never fell short. The level of satisfaction he could deliver to all on his to-do list kept him off the beware lists of other women. Even with all the rumors swirling around Hollywood about being a complete womanizer and sex addict. The fact of the matter was this actually only helped him. He was a sex god in most women's eyes in the movie screen world. Any woman who was lucky enough to be seen on his arm for longer than one night was hated and considered a goddess to all the rest prior. Being more than a one-night stand with Spencer was an honor, a privilege given to not many. Cassie, of course, got to spend Christmas with him, but he wanted to meet her family and put her on a pedestal above all the rest. It was the talk of the movie set community; Spencer Doyle was actually dating a girl and wanted to meet her family. This made all the others willing to sleep their way up on the screen lose all hope and search for new opportunities and womanizers. Spencer had to stay focused on only Cassie, so he made her exclusive, with a few exceptions along the way, of course. This made Cassie feel so special and loved. When a sexy man appears in a pair of tight Levi's, a six-pack poking through a T-shirt, with a wicked smile and bad habits, women get in line. Most women are not stupid and can see through most men, but nonetheless, they, too, will get in line. Women like bad boys that like to pretend; it's the ultimate sexual attraction. Maybe it has to do with control or feeling like they won over other women; it's an "Ah look, he picked me" kind of a deal. Either way, it's the way of the world, whether admitted or not, and Demons flourish in these situations and can play reckless games of power and deceit. Spencer knew he was holding all the power in the world in his pants. All he had to do was smile and make them feel as though they were complete on his arm, safe in his embrace, and satisfied in his bed. All of which became his second nature and would succeed every single time. Cassie was blind to all this and only felt what he wanted her to feel when he wanted her to feel it. He had absolute power over her, and she would die before giving him or the career opportunities up. Cassie was under Spencer's evil trance and had no chance of winning this chess game she was unaware she was playing. Spencer was, in all his immoral glory, playing the best strategic game of chess in his life. Smitty was waiting for him in Hell, and he knew what would happen to him in the case of him not winning. There wasn't a day or second that went by that Spencer didn't remind Cassie of her need for him. He was like heroin to her; she had to have him or would go into uttermost withdrawals. They would have sex just about everywhere, and the flight to Alaska was no different; they joined the Mile High Club several times on the way there. They irritated all the other passengers at first but then made them envious by the time the flight ended. The passion between them made those romance novels sold on the endcaps of grocery stores look tame in comparison. Heather and the Summers were up for one heck of a battle with this stranger and the spells he had Cassie under. How could Heather ever get Cassie to see the glimmer of light instead of the drug-like addiction to his sexy darkness?

Penelope would be of no help, for she still had her own journey to figure out, and Cassie's newfound situation was way above her head.

CHAPTER 21

Heather takes two steps back after Spencer lets go of her, embraced in his arm with such force it started to hurt her. Asher, Cruz, and Grayson start to walk towards Heather with aggression and seriousness. Heather holds up her hand, and the three boys stop in their tracks. Dean was still standing behind Heather with his arms crossed, and he had not moved an inch. Penelope was fluttering around in excitement and wasn't picking up on the vibe at all; of course, this was Cassie and her new handsome boyfriend. Penelope takes Cassie and Spencer by the hands and leads them over to the Tahoe. She begins to help them load their Louis Vuitton luggage into the hatchback. Heather, her sons, and Dean are now standing alone, watching the three of them, hand in hand, walking towards the truck. All were laughing and looking so happy when Spencer turned around and gave them a revolting smile as if saying he's already winning. Dean, Asher, Cruz, and Grayson all turn and look at Heather. Heather was standing tall and confident, but her face looked sad and distressed. For she knew she would have to destroy her sister Cassie's world and everything that she thought it was. The utter hurt and endless sadness never stop for Guardian Angels. They wear this on their faces and hold this in their souls like anchors sitting on the ocean floor forty-seven meters deep. Dean then breaks the barrier of silence among them all and asks Heather what Spencer said to her when he whispered in her ear. Heather turned, looked at Dean with a more driven look than he had ever witnessed her express to him, and she said, "Spencer Doyle is our Christmas present from Smitty." Dean and all three of their sons look back at Penelope, Cassie, and their present from Smitty, Spencer Doyle. Dean then grabs Heather's hand and says, "Well, Smitty was never a good gift giver," and they all begin to walk towards the darkness they see getting into the vehicle. The Summers know that they will have to play Spencer's chess game and are all gearing up for the what's next move on the board. Each move will have to be done with such precision and thought. Spencer was a crafty Demon, not as old and powerful as Smitty, but he had swagger and suaveness about him that made him very dangerous. He was persuasive and cunning, especially with women. He now had two women that Heather cared about under his spell. First Cassie and now Penelope. Even though she had just met him, the spell was already cast, and Penelope was wearing it like a fur coat around her body, feeling all nice and cozy. This guy was good, and he was out to win. The Summers reached the vehicle, and as they were about to open the doors and get in, Spencer jumped out, opening the door for Heather. He was flexing once again how he was in control. Heather gave him her best poker face, and as he went to shut the door, she smiled at Spencer and whispered, "Game On." Spencer smiled back with his obnoxiously eye-catching smile and replied with only one sinful word, "Torngarsuk." Torngarsuk is the Inuit translation for the word Demon.

CHAPTER 22

Heather had lived her entire life surrounded by an evil force destined to ruin every single holiday imaginable; this Christmas would be no different. It would seem impossible for others to have a Demon under the same roof for Christmas of all holidays, but not for Heather. She was used to this sort of dysfunction, and it was part of her norm to be a Guardian Angel. She knew that Smitty had purposely sent Spencer for Christmas; it was his specialty, dampening holidays with his soggy and evil rains of ruin. Heather had to keep her wits and cool about her; although she wasn't scared of Spencer, she was scared for her sister Cassie. She knew no matter what the outcome was going to be, breaking Cassie's heart would all have to be part of it. There was no way around it; Cassie would not be able to be convinced that she could live without the heroin she was fully and one hundred percent addicted to. Heather knew trying to get Cassie to see even the smallest glimmer of light was not realistic. Again, the task and assignments of the Guardian Angels may not always seem beneficial to everyone involved. Sometimes deep hurt and hard life changes have to be made in the best interest of the journey they are meant to pursue. Ultimately, it's exactly how things were meant to play out in everyone's life. Cassie and Spencer stayed in their bedroom for the majority of the first night in the cabin. They could hear them giggling and laughing most of the night. Penelope thought it was cute, the love-struck couple enjoying their time. Penelope just liked seeing Cassie happy and laughing. Heather, on the other hand, knew what Spencer was doing and why he was doing it. Torment, pure and utter torment to Heather and to the rest of her family who Shined and Dean the Seer. The first morning at breakfast, Spencer made sure to come down in only his tight white Versace boxers. Clearly, he was used to using this as a weapon, but the Summers were not impressed with it at all. Penelope turned bright red in embarrassment at the sight that was now eye level with her at the fridge as she tried to enjoy her coffee at the table. Dean, at the stove, flipping eggs, turns and looks at Spencer, swigging the orange juice straight from the container, not bothering to pour it into a glass like a normal person. Dean shakes his head and asks, "Spencer, would you like a glass for that orange juice, buddy?" Spencer replies, "No, I plan on drinking the whole thing; not necessary." Dean then laughs and says, "Pants must not be necessary either, huh?" Spencer, smiling, takes the carton of orange juice and his half-naked chiseled body up the staircase, and they soon hear Cassie laughing and giggling again. Penelope comments, "How nice it would be to be young and in love." Heather shakes her head and tells her mother, "He's not a catch for Cassie. He's a Demon mother." Penelope is taken aback and completely in shock by what Heather has just revealed to her. Says, "You can't be serious?" With anguish in her voice, Heather says, "I am afraid so, Mother. He has been sent by Smitty." Penelope, not having heard that name spoken in a while, feels a dark fear and regret in her soul. She had a million things running through her head all at once. The only thing she could muster up was the words, "Oh no, not again." Heather knew by Penelope's long-distance stare that it was all rushing back to her. All four decades of abuse and still freshly half-closed wounds were instantly surface level. Penelope's scars would forever remain with her for the rest of her life; how she chose to deal with them would be her true spiritual journey. Dean stopped what he was doing and joined the conversation at the breakfast table. Penelope looked up at him and asked if he also knew about Spencer. Heather reminded Penelope that Dean was a Seer and could see the Shine like Heather and their three sons. So yes, Dean is aware of the situation at hand, Mother, Heather, said to Penelope. Penelope, in complete confused shock, asks Heather what is she going to do. Heather replies that the only thing she can do is finish her assignment, and this must be it. She thought that Smitty was her assignment for the longest time. It turns out she was only a small piece in that task, and this must be her true task at hand. Guardian angels know who they are to guard towards their spiritual journey, but their assignments are not entirely known till they present themselves. It's just how it is, and Guardian Angels are not meant to question any order of how the divine puzzle pieces are to be placed or when they are to be dealt with. Heather was Penelope's Guardian Angel, who guided her towards her spiritual journey. Heather unknowingly brought Dean into their lives to complete a task that was never meant to be Heather's. Dean the Seer was always meant to send Smitty back to the place he was never supposed to leave. Heather still had an assignment to complete, and this must be what she and her celestial soldiers were always meant to take on and destroy. Spencer and Cassie finally went downstairs late that afternoon and joined the rest of the family, sitting by the fire, reading, and playing with the French Bull Dogs. As Spencer rounds the corner, the Frenchie start to growl and bark, not liking what they feel coming towards them. Heather and Dean pick the dogs up and put them in their bedroom. Spencer and Cassie sit down next to Asher on the Couch, who removes himself and goes and sits on the stone bench in front of the crackling fireplace. Cruz and Grayson are on the loveseat across from them. Cruz speaks up and says to Cassie: "So, how did you meet this tall, dark, and handsome man Auntie Cass?" Cassie smiles and begins to go on and on about how they met at some glamorous party and how Spencer invited her to one of his movie sets. She continues to regale in all the memories of their first dates and so on. Everyone in the room is not hearing a single word she is saying; instead, all of them, including Penelope, have their eyes on Spencer. He notices, and he, too just stares back at each and every one of them with warning signs in his deep dark eyes. Cassie then says, "Hello, is anyone even listening to me?" Penelope then chimes in and says, "Yes, of course, dear; we are just all surprised, is all." Cassie gets done spilling her love-struck guts and says she needs a drink, and leaves the room to pour herself a whiskey in the kitchen. That left Spencer alone in the room where all eyes were on him, and no one was smiling. Spencer then takes the opportunity to say how he sure wished he could have met Smitty, Cassie talks about him all the time, and she's not sure why he hasn't called. Heather then sees Cassie returning to the room and speaks up, saying, "Smitty was always a selfish man who only cared about himself. So, it's no surprise he hasn't tried to call anyone." Penelope remains silent now, staring at the crackling fire. Cassie then says, "So, no one has heard from him yet?" Dean starts adding wood to the fire, and the boys remove themselves to retrieve more wood from the outside deck. Heather begins to tell Cassie that they are better off with him doing his own thing, and Cassie somewhat agrees and says, "Yeah, I guess so." Spencer butts in and says, "But wouldn't you like to at least know he's ok, Cassie? Maybe you should put out a missing person's report." Penelope looks at Heather with a terrified look on her face. Heather then tells Spencer that maybe he should mind his own business with family matters that are not of his concern. Cassie then chimes in and says, "Well, Heather, they are of his concern because we are officially engaged, and he's part of the family." Cassie then jumps up, showing off her huge diamond. She is chattering nonstop about where they got the ring, how the ring had been specially designed, and how it was a one-of-a-kind yellow-cut three-carat diamond. Heather takes a deep breath and gives Penelope the look of just play along mother. Penelope refutably smiles and says well, congratulations, I guess. This is why we didn't tell you

Spencer was joining us for Christmas; we wanted it to be a big surprise. Spencer now has his arms crossed and smirks at everyone in the room with a "Beat that" game face. He had just made his first chess move, and it was a doozy. Heather knew at that moment that she would have to tell Cassie the truth about Smitty. Cassie would most definitely want Smitty to walk her down the aisle and would be on the hunt for him as soon as possible. Spencer was purposely making things uncomfortable for Penelope and the Summers. That is exactly how Demons always start their chess games. Make everyone self-doubting lunatics and get loved ones to turn on each other. It's a great start position for Demons to weaken their opponents without them noticing what is unfolding in front of them. This way, all the blame and years of resentment go toward their loved ones and each other, not toward the actual mastermind of the chess game. It's the ultimate distraction for them to achieve their end game. Spencer knew this move would be the perfect distraction for Heather and Penelope to be focused on Cassie's feelings rather than defeating him. Spencer underestimated Heather and her feelings for

Cassie. Although Heather never wanted to hurt her sister, if it meant saving her family and doing her divine task at hand, that would certainly come first. Cassie, clueless about the situation, would never believe them anyways, and Spencer knew this and used it to his advantage. Demons also strive for hate; they adore when humans show others hate and disgust. It's like having a cold brew on a hot day for them to sit back and enjoy. Hate definitely quenches their thirst for destruction and devastation. It gives them a little buzz and keeps their vile goals fresh and hydrated. All Heather can say when Cassie shows her the huge beastly ring is, wow. Heather still has her eyes on Spencer the entire time, and she knows she has the next move, and it better be a good one. Spencer is playing with fire, and he loves it. Heather then says to Cassie maybe she should consider holding the ceremony in the church where she and Dean were married. Spencer tilts his head to the side and says back to Heather, "I think Vegas is more our style." Heather then says to Spencer yep, sin city does seem more up your alley. Cassie then becomes aware of the tension between her sister and her fiancé and says, "Oh come on, are we already having family wedding arguments?" Spencer laughs and says, "Of course not; your sister is just being honest with you about her wishes." Penelope then interrupts and states that she thinks they shouldn't rush into things and there's nothing wrong with staying engaged for a while to get to know each other. Cassie then hugs her mother and says, "Don't worry, Mother, I know exactly who Spence is, and we are perfect for each other." Heather rolls her eyes at Penelope, and just then, Asher, Cruz, and Grayson return with bundles of firewood in their arms. They can tell by the look on Dean's face that they just missed something, and Grayson says to Cassie, "Ok Auntie Cassie, what did we miss?" Cassie whips out her hand and shows all of Heather's three Shining sons her newly announced engagement news. The boys all look at each other and then at Spencer, who is eagerly awaiting their response. Just then, they all three walked over to Spencer, picked him up from the slumber he was in on the couch, and Asher said, "Looks like someone needs to cool down." They haul him through the cabin's front door and throw him in the first snow bank they find off the deck. He lands hard and sinks deep into a six-foot-deep snow bank. Cassie thinking this is just her silly nephews doing an early bachelor party like tradition is laughing and running after them, telling them to stop. Spencer gets himself out of the snow bank looking like Frosty himself and says all you shits will pay for this, as Cassie kisses his snowy, wet cheek telling him it's just family tradition and all in good family fun. Spencer smiles at Asher, Cruz, and Grayson and says, "Well, I guess you got me, but you boys better sleep with one eye open in a serious tone of voice." Asher, Cruz, and Grayson all head back in the house laughing and give Dean and Heather a shrug, saying, "He had it coming." Heather knew Spencer had lots of game left to play, and this would be a vertical strategic battle up a very steep and dangerous mountain. Smitty was an old and powerful Demon, but Spencer was a younger, more cunning Demon.

CHAPTER 23

Christmas was only a week away, and Heather knew she was on borrowed time to get her sister Cassie away from her new fiancé Spencer Doyle the Demon sent by Smitty. Heather decided to take Spencer and Cassie into town with her to get a few extra things for Christmas dinner. Heather knew part of her army was in town, and maybe he could assist her in this unwaning task at hand. The three of them walked into the Eagles Landing, Heather in the lead, with Cassie following her. Nanook was restocking the canned goods in aisle three when he first saw Heather and Cassie. As he walks towards them, he then sees Spencer entering the store. His face drops, and his wrinkles begin to speak volumes to Heather. Cassie thinking he's just some weird crazy old Eskimo, walks over and joins Spencer. Heather and Nanook make eye contact and have an entire conversation without speaking. Nanook knows who Spencer is and knows who now who Cassie is. Heather knows he knows, and they begin to walk toward the freezer section of the Grocery store while Spencer and Cassie head toward the bread aisle. Spencer kept his eyes on Nanook and Heather as they walk away, and Spencer knows what Nanook truly is. He now knows why Heather wanted them to come with him and what Heather's next move may be. He tells Cassie to go find the buns that they needed in the bread aisle, and he walks to the end of the aisle, where he could see Nanook and Heather standing. He stays and watches them as they continue to walk to the back of the stock room at the end of the aisle. Cassie then comes up behind Spencer and asks him what the heck he was doing; they had a whole list to look for. Heather and Nanook reach the Grocery Store's back door and exit together. Nanook has a look of fear on his face; this was the first time Heather saw him nervous. Nanook, the confident, tough Shaman who rarely spoke, begins speaking very fast and with great intent. He began telling Heather that Spencer is a Demon messenger, one of the worst of his kind. Heather agrees with Nanook and tells him she knows. Nanook then continued to explain to Heather what a messenger from Hell truly meant in his culture. "Heather, he is an Ijiraq. This is a Demon who can shapeshift into arctic animals at will. The only way you can tell it is an Ijiraq is by their red eyes." said Nanook. They are unable to hide their red eyes when they shapeshift. These are very dangerous Demons who can disguise themselves in their surroundings. Nanook then continued explaining to Heather how he would likely shift into a black wolf. Nanook could see other spirit animals, including Demons who were evil spirit animals to the Inuit culture. Nanook, the Shaman that he was, could see what animal Spencer would more than likely shape-shift into. Smitty sent this type of Demon due to the location of Nome and the accessibility to shapeshift into an arctic animal. Heather was going to battle not only with a malevolent Demon but one that could shapeshift and disguise itself into a fierce vicarious animal. Heather was not prepared for this, and Nanook made sure she was aware of what type of Demon, her family and she was up against. Heather, now entirely aware of Spencer's up-and-coming violent chess moves, could up her game with Nanook. Nanook said, "It would likely happen on the full moon that was coming up on Christmas Eve. Demons that shapeshift into black wolves tend to like full moons." Nanook went on to explain that Spencer would have his most power under a full moon and to beware that night.

CHAPTER 24

Nanook was a widower and lost his wife of many decades to cancer. He never could get over that; even as a Shaman, some things were never meant to be cured, and fate is fate. He had cured many people throughout his life as a medicine man in his tribe, but he couldn't save his own wife. These were Nanook's Demons that kept him awake at night. Nanook's wife could never have children, so it was always just her and Nanook. After she passed, Nanook lost himself in being a Shaman and taking care of the tribes' children and community. There was a little boy that was brought to his attention years prior by his very upset and worried mother. The little boy was said to be possessed by a Demon, and his mother wanted Nanook to banish the Demon from her only son. Nanook traveled deep into the wilderness where this child and his mother lived. He rode a snow machine till he finally had to walk with snowshoes to reach their tiny little cabin deep in the Alaskan wilderness. The cabin didn't have power. It was lit by the fire and candles flickering in the windows. Nanook had dealt with many cases of possession in his lifetime, but for some reason, he knew this would be a case that he wouldn't be able to unsee. The tribal people had warned Nanook of what they had witnessed the boy doing, and Nanook knew he had his work cut out for him. As he approached the cabin, he could hear growling sounds and something inside the cabin mumbling words in tongues. It didn't sound like a child, let alone a human. He knocked three times on the door when the homemade log door cracked open, and the mother was peeking out at Nanook. He explained he was the Shaman she had requested, and his name was Nanook. She reluctantly opened the cabin door, and as she did, all the candles blew out simultaneously, but there was no wind that night. It was a brisk cold winter's evening, and the snow was crisp with sound but no wind. The fire lighting the little trapper's cabin was all that illuminated the room at that point. The boy's mother stepped aside, letting Nanook to enter the one-room cabin. He could see a boy across the room, who seemed about ten years old. He was tied to a bed in the corner of the one-room cabin. His hands were tied, and so were his feet. His wrists and ankles were bleeding from the rope that had been digging into his flesh and tearing it wide open with every pull and tug. Nanook sat down on the one chair that was in front of a table by the front door. He began to take off his snow shoes and remove items from a knapsack he had brought with him. In the reindeer knapsack were a mask with horns, huge ivory carved hands, and a ceremonial parka and boots. Each item he removed angered the little boy that was no longer a little boy. The growls got louder, and the mumbling got meaner and faster. The mother was begging Nanook not to leave at this point, and he sat her down and reassured her he wasn't going anywhere and to stay strong for her son. Nanook told her to sing and don't stop no matter what. It was for her son's sake, and sing like his life depended on it. Inuit use a vocal style of language called Inuktitut; the translation is throat singing. Nanook then dresses as the boy becomes almost unrecognizable in anger and begins foaming at the mouth. The mother continues to sing, but Nanook can hear sobbing in her song. He approaches the side of the boy's bed, looking very much a fright himself in his Demon-banishing clothing and mask. The boy begins to laugh a deep coarse manly laugh, not a laugh of a ten-year-old. Nanook begins his Shaman prayers and rituals; meanwhile, the Demon was expressing himself more and more to Nanook. Just then, the boy snaps the ropes on his hands, setting the top half of his body free, and lunges towards Nanook with such force the entire bed moves with him. Nanook takes a step back and continues; as he begins for a second time, the boy snaps his tied-up legs free, throws himself up to the corner of the cabin, and is now balancing on the ceiling six feet above Nanook. The boy's mother is now on her feet and ready to run out the door at a moment's notice. Nanook starts speaking and singing much louder and much faster; although he is wearing a huge mask, his voice resonates throughout the entire cabin in an echoing fashion. The boy, still looking down at Nanook and his mother, begins to crawl on the cabin's ceiling towards the door when Nanook says two last

Shaman prayers, and the boy's body drops from the ceiling. The boy lands on the cabin floor, not speaking and not moving. The mother goes to the aid of her son, now helpless, looking and lying on the cold floor half naked. Nanook yells no, stop, don't approach him. Just then, the little boy jumped on his mother with his hands around her neck, choking her. Nanook drops his ivory-carved ginormous sharp gloves, pulls the boy off his mother with his bare hands, and throws him on the bed in the corner. Taking off any part of the Shamans Exorcist garments is a huge risk to a Shaman's ability to protect themselves. They believe if they are not fully covered and expose a part of their body to a Demon, they risk becoming possessed themselves. As Nanook was trying to quickly get his ivory hands back over his actual hands, the boy lunged forward once again, only this time the boy lunged right into one of the razor-sharp ivory carved fingers that is about two feet long. The ivory finger penetrates straight into the boy's heart, Nanook quickly removes his mask and tries to remove the ivory finger from the boy's little chest but knows that it's too late, and there is no help for miles. The mother begins to scream, runs to her son crying, and becomes inconsolable. For she knew that her son was already gone weeks ago, but this finalized it for her. Nanook puts one finger on either side of the ivory spear now deep in the boy's chest. Nanook slowly begins to pull the hand from the boy's chest, and the blood rushes out and fills the cabin floor with the scent of putrid-smelling metallics. The Demon gives out one last foul laugh and says with a blood-filled throat, "I win." Nanook jumps back, dropping the boy. He took the boy's mother by her hand and stood her up. They said some prayers. Nanook explained to her that her son was gone before he even arrived, and they now had to go. Nanook knew the only way to truly know if the Demon was gone was to set it on fire and burn the cabin down. The mother was aware of this, so she and Nanook took the small can of gasoline she had for her snow machine and poured it all around the cabin. Nanook told the boy's mother to wait outside; Nanook took the quilt off the bed, wrapped the boy's limp body up in it like a tight burial cocoon, and poured the remainder of the gasoline on the quilt. He took logs from the fire and put them in each corner of the cabin, setting it ablaze before walking outside with his knap sack and snow shoes. He had the boy's mother put his snow shoes on, and they began to walk away from the cabin, now engulfed in flames and crumbling under pressure. There was nothing more Nanook or his mother could do for the little Inuit child taken over by an old and powerful Demon. They both knew they had done everything they could for him. The sadness from that night would remain in Nanook's heart and soul for all his remaining years on this Earth. Even though it wasn't anyone's fault but the Demons, it still destroyed that mother's faith and Nanook's faith in himself for the rest of his life. In a way, the Demon won by destroying a part of their souls that night in that cabin. When they reached the little town of Nome, both brokenhearted and in utter distress, the boy's mother thanked Nanook for saving her and her son. Nanook was confused because he didn't think he saved her son, rather quite the opposite, but the mother said you did save him from being kidnapped by a Demon. You sent him to a better place with protection. She then told Nanook that a respected tribal member had raped her as a young girl and that the little boy was the result. She was so ashamed of being raped, assuming it was her fault that she never told anyone about the assault. She didn't think anyone would believe her since her rapist was a very respected father and a married member of the tribe. She raised the little boy in the little trapper's cabin her grandmother had given her, with no power for ten years. The boy started to show signs of possession around seven, but she knew no one would believe that either. She lived with her Demons in her soul and a Demon in the woods for several years, isolated and alone. Her grandmother was her only family, and she had passed away when the boy was two years old, so she never had a chance to tell her or get help from her. Not a burden she ever wanted to place on her sickly elderly grandmother, but one she always wished she had. Her grandmother was a medicine woman for the tribe, also very respected, and maybe could have done something. Or maybe not; that's how men with power get away with even murder. He knew she would be intimidated and scared to report him. She would have to see him around town with his family, and he would glance over, smile, and then go on his merry way with his wife and children. He would visit her occasionally at her cabin and bring her food and supplies but would expect favors in return, willingly or not willingly; either way didn't matter to him. She was never so happy to see that cabin burn to the ground. Now she could start a new life, away from Nome and away from him. Nanook always suspected this was the case with her, and he figured he was pretty sure who the powerful man was she was talking about. He reached inside his pants pocket and pulled out a snow-damp wad of cash, all hundred-dollar bills. He handed her the cash and said he would tell everyone the mother and son died in the cabin fire that night. In a way, he wouldn't be fully wrong, for a piece of her did burn up in that cabin that cold, bitter, cruel winter night. Nome wasn't known for its grand investigations into death scenarios, so no one would question it otherwise. As they both walked in opposite directions that dark winter night, Nanook knew he would never see her again and for this, he was blissful for her. Delighted that maybe for the first time, she could go and spread her wings and fly. For

Nanook knew she was so much more than an abused young woman with Demons in her soul. She, too, like her grandmother, was always meant to become a well-respected medicine woman of her tribe and didn't know it. She was never given a chance in life and was dealt a dead man's hand. She was unable to know about her full potential in life, and for this, Nanook was beyond sorrowful. Although she never practiced her skills with strangers, down in her heart, she always knew there was something special about herself, and someday she would fly like an Eagle and find her way. Until then, her soul and mind required healing, and leaving Nome was her only option for now. Nanook gave one last look back as she started to disappear in the fog of snow, and the lack of visibility became less and less. Nanook said "Fly high Ahnah." Ahnah was the mother's name. This meant "Wise woman," the Inuit goddess of fertility and childbirth. Ahnah's grandmother had told her many things before she passed, and so Ahnah was not blind to her abilities, just not confident and sure of herself enough to know she was so much more. Ahnah had named her son Tattuk, the Inuit word for dark spirit. She knew the moment he was born that there was something mysterious and dark about her newborn baby son born out of sin. She delivered him alone in her cabin in the deep-set forest one fall day on Friday the thirteenth.

CHAPTER 25

The wind began to pick up, and the snow started to blow and fill in the snow machine and snow shoe tracks. Nanook knew there would be no trace of them in or out of that cabin for anyone to assume otherwise. The tribe knew of her Demon troubles with her son and would assume that she just burned the cabin down with them both in it to try to set them both free of their Demons. Death and missing people in Nome are common occurrences with no impending investigations to intercede. Over eleven thousand people are unexplainably missing in Nome alone. With no road systems in or out of the city, this seems not very logical; non the less, it is what it is. Nanook reported the fire that morning. The authorities all went out to the cabin the next morning after the storm, which was now just a pile of burnt ash highlighted with white snow all around it as if it was a burial ground. There in among the people sent out to investigate the accident, for that's what they would call it, was him. The man that abused Ahnah as a young girl. The man who tortured that poor woman for most of her life, standing there looking down at what used to be a historic trapper's cabin. Although Ahnah never told him who it was, Nanook knew it was him. He stood there watching this poor excuse of a human being pretending to be saddened like the others around him, but Nanook knew otherwise. He knew he was glad she was gone along with his son; he never claimed. His chances of being exposed, in his mind, were now gone, and he could sleep easier at night with his lies and evilness. Nanook stood there with pure resentment for this man, a respected member of the community and tribe. His mind drifted back to all the missing young girls in Nome, with no explanation of their whereabouts. Something in his Shaman soul told him that this evil and powerful man had something to do with all the disappearing Inuit girls, but how could he prove it? For Nanook could see a dark cloud of haze and dust surrounding him. He could also see a hint of red in his eyes if he looked at the man just right. This man was the acting Mayor of Nome. Nanook knew now that the only reason why Ahnah didn't go missing like all the others was for the mere fact that she was a medicine woman, just as her grandmother was. Something he couldn't fully win against, like the other innocent girls who he raped and made vanish in thin air as if they never existed at all. There is no trace, no clues, no speck of evidence to support their kidnappings. Even though the state of Alaska believed that this was the work of a serial killer. The FBI led an investigation but found that alcohol abuse and the dangers of Alaska's wilderness were most likely to blame. Eventually, they all were tagged as runaways and young girls with mental illnesses and substance abuse issues. The Inuit parents and friends of these missing girls knew otherwise, but in such an isolated town with minimal resources, there was only so much they could do. Once the FBI closed its chapter on the investigations, the tribe was forced to move forward. There was a total of over thirty teenage girls that had all gone unexplainably missing throughout his years as Mayor of Nome. All the missing girls were from Nome and the surrounding villages and were all between the ages of thirteen to seventeen years old. Nome was a mysterious place without all the missing girls, making it even more surreptitious and covert to all the newcomers, including the Summers. Nanook always knew what the Mayor of Nome truly was, being the only Shaman of the tribe and able to see things most cannot. But if the FBI couldn't prove it, how would Nanook ever be able to. Serial Killers usually are only caught when they want to be; it's a game for them that they win till they get bored with it. Getting themselves caught gives them a whole new game to play, challenging law enforcement to prove it. They are Demons walking among the people on Earth, playing wicked chess games with the goodness and purity of the people around them. In the Mayor's case, he had power in his position with local law enforcement and the FBI. As a matter of fact, it was the mayor who pushed for the FBI to open an investigation in the town of Nome regarding the missing teenage girls. He was seen at press conferences with the FBI saying it's a tragedy and darn shame that nothing has been done about it till now. All part of his chess game and a brand-new challenge. Serial Killers are game players and are always up for a new challenge; this is what fuels their passions for murder and mayhem. It has been said that people will walk past at least thirty-six serial killers in their lifetime. Since the 1980's, there are still over two hundred thousand unsolved serial killer cases in the United States alone. Seventy percent of all serial killings happen in the United States. There are four types of serial killers' mission-orientated, visionary, control-orientated, and hedonistic. The mayor was a visionary and a power-control serial killer who could attribute his killings to visions or voices directing him to perform his acts of violence. Ted Bundy was also a power-control type of serial killer who was eventually caught and confessed to thirty murders of young girls in seven states across the U.S.

CHAPTER 26

The ride home after the trip to the Eagle's Landing with Cassie and Spencer was interesting. Cassie was nonstop about how she couldn't imagine why anyone would want to live in Nome. Spencer was quiet and just stared at Heather in the rear-view mirror the entire drive back. Heather had flexed on him with Nanook the Shaman, so he would have to change up some of his well-thought-out plans. He was agitated with this, and Heather could see it in his dark eyes, glaring her down in the mirror. When they finally reached the cabin, Spencer asked Heather, "Do you guys see many bears around here." Heather replied hesitantly, knowing the newfound information that Nanook had just shared with her. She said, "Yes, Spencer, this is Alaska, of course, we see bears all the time." Spencer chuckled and said "Perfect, I have always wanted to have an encounter with a grizzly bear in

Alaska." Heather reminds Spencer that the bears are all in hibernation this time of year, so good luck. Cassie then chimed in, "What are you talking about, why would you ever want to see one of those beasts." Spencer then grabbed Cassie, pulling her tight against his well-chiseled chest, and said "Because I am a grizzly bear that doesn't hibernate and would like to get back to my animal instincts, babe." Cassie slaps his chest and laughs, telling him not in front of my sister. Spencer says, "Heather can handle it, can't you, Heather?" Heather looks at Cassie, smiles, and says, "Bears don't scare me; Cassie, people do." Cassie rolls her eyes and shakes her head, heading for the front door of the cabin. Spencer and Heather's eyes meet, and she knows at that moment the game is about to be set forth in an uncontrollable, fast-forward motion. Spencer was sent there for revenge, and it would get nasty. Heather was not scared for herself but for her sister, who she assumed would be his first plan of attack. Dean, Asher, Cruz, and Grayson were waiting for them as they walked into the cabin with hands full of grocery bags. Dean then says to Spencer, "Up for a boy's day of adventure, buddy?"

Spencer replies he is always up for an adventure. Dean's three sons smile and start getting their artic boots and Canadian Goose jackets and gloves on. Cruz says to Spencer, "Better dress warm; the Alaskan cold can creep up on a person." Asher laughs and says, "We sure would hate for you to freeze off your tools." Grayson joins in and says, "Tools, what tools?" Not reacting to any of it, Spencer starts to get dressed in silence. He was a hard egg to crack, and the boys all picked up that ruffling his feathers wouldn't be an easy task. Spencer kisses Cassie goodbye, and she yells out to her brother-in-law Dean and her three nephews to take it easy on him. Spencer turns to Cassie and replies, "You mean for me to take it easy on them, right babe?" Cassie smiles and says yes, of course, that's what I meant. They all hop on the five snow machines lined up on the side of the cabin. Dean asked Spencer if he had ever driven one before, and Spencer said, "No, but I got this." Dean shrugs and says, "Alrighty, then let's go." The four of them speed away, leaving Spencer in their snow-dusty cloud. Spencer soon catches up to the gang, and they speed across the land to a trailhead, where they jump on and head up the mountainside. It had just snowed the night before, so the fresh powder was perfect for their adventure. Since they were all wearing snow goggles, their eyes were shielded, but the four watched Spencer closely. Dean stopped and pointed out a pack of wolf tracks alongside the trail as they climbed up the snow-filled mountain trail. He knew there would be a fresh kill around with the pack all together and surrounding the area. Dean was armed under his thick winter Goose jacket. It sat on his chest, ready and willing to aid if need be. Asher, Cruz, and Grayson were also armed with grizzly guns under their jackets. They were not concealing them from the weather but from Spencer. They were aware that, more than likely, a gun wouldn't kill him since he was a Fallen Angel. He would have to be destroyed with a sacred Angel blade or some sort of divine weapon. Regardless, none of them were going into the vast Alaskan wilderness without some sort of protection against him. Violet's Archangel Blade, which she had Penelope give to Heather, was safely in its case in Heather's closet back at the cabin. The same Angel Blade that Dean had used to destroy Smitty lay patiently waiting for its next divine task at hand. The red velvet case that held the blade in perfect position was ancient looking and deadly. It looked like it had just been dug up for Heather, even though that was in the past. Dean knew from his visions today was not the day that he would need it. Heather had made a hidden cabinet in her closet in the cabin. The logs would pop out when pushed just right, and inside the hidden cabinet, it would appear. That was the only thing in that hidden cabinet. Heather, Cassie, and Penelope decided to make Christmas cookies while the men were gone on their adventure. Something the girls remembered their mother doing when they were children. They put on Kenny G Christmas music, and Cassie began listing off her favorite cookies and what they all should make. Penelope grabbed Cassie's arm and said, "Hey, we really need to have a sister-to-sister talk." Cassie, worried, slowly began to sit down on the kitchen chair. Penelope also sat down across from her. Heather began by saying, "You know we only want you to be happy and safe." Cassie says, "Yes, of course." "Well," Penelope begins to say, "Do you believe in Heaven and Hell, Cassie?" Cassie gets a weird look and says, "Yeah, I guess so; why?" "Well, Cassie, we need to tell you something, and it may sound crazy to you, but please keep an open mind." Cassie sits still and stiff as a board listening to Heather and watching Penelope's reactions. Heather takes a deep breath and begins to explain to Cassie. "Cassie, there are Guardian Angels that walk among us and Fallen Angels that also walk among us." Cassie begins to chuckle but then sees the serious face on both her mother and sister. Penelope speaks up and says, "Cassie, please listen to Heather." Cassie looks back at Heather, and she continues. "Smitty was a Fallen Angel who was never meant to walk among the people on Earth. Satan tortured him, sent him to Earth to possess a person, and cause death and destruction." Cassie tries to process all that Heather is saying as she sees tears roll down Penelope's face. Penelope did not cry very often, or at least never let anyone see her cry. She saw it as a form of weakness; she always wanted to uphold a tough image. That would for sure tell everyone who witnessed her crying otherwise. Cassie knew at that moment what Heather was saying was not a joke and she was serious.

"Cassie," Penelope said, "Heather is a Guardian Angel sent here to protect me, well us." Cassie looks back at Heather with an utmost confused look on her face. She then asks, "Is that why Smitty always treated you so badly, Heather?" "Yes," said Heather, "He was threatened by the Shine." Cassie then asked, "What is the Shine?" Heather said "It's a characteristic that only others who Shine can see. It's a radiant, shimmering glow that resonates from all who Shine." Penelope then adds, "Dean can see it." Heather continues telling Cassie that Dean can see it because he is a Seer with divine visions and has crystal ball-like capabilities for some future events. Cassie sits back in her chair in shock, trying to process the crazy information her sister and mother are dumping on her. Cassie then asks Heather, "Where is Smitty?" "He is gone and back where he never should have left in the first place." Tears start to roll down Cassie's face as she digests what seem like razor blades down her throat as her emotions all build up. She always knew that Smitty was a mean man watching how he mistreated her sister Heather and abused her mother, but she never thought he was this. Heather wiped a tear from

Cassie's cheek and says "Cassie, Smitty was a very ancient and powerful Demon who had to be dealt with." Penelope then adds, "Asher, Cruz, and Grayson are also Guardian Angels sent to aid Heather and be part of her divine army here on Earth." Cassie shakes her head and becomes angry; all part of the stages of processing unimaginable information for a person. "Why didn't you tell me all this? Why are you telling me all this now?" Penelope and Heather look at each other, thinking well, here goes nothing. Heather says, "Cassie, Spencer is playing you and using you to get at me and my family." Cassie stands up, about ready to storm out of the room; when Penelope says, "Sit down, Cassie," very sternly. Cassie reluctantly sits back down with her arms now crossed on her chest as a form of protection against the information coming her way. "How do you know this," asks Cassie. "Because he told me so, Cassie. He whispered something in my ear at the airport to let me know that he had been sent for revenge by Smitty." "What did he say?" Cassie asked. "It doesn't matter. You wouldn't understand the connection just know it was something only Smitty would know." Heather then drops the bomb and says, "Cassie Spencer shines malevolent and is a Fallen Angel." Cassie being Cassie replies with, "Why do all the super sexy men always seem to have something wrong with them." Heather gives Cassie a look of, that's all you got out of this conversation. Cassie then asks, "Who 'dealt' with Smitty?" Heather replies, "That doesn't matter either," saving Dean from any unnecessary judgment that would be passed on to him from Cassie. Penelope chimes in that Heather and her family saved her, or Smitty would have killed her eventually. "Well, I guess Dean will have to walk me down the aisle then, huh?" Heather says, "Cassie, you can't marry Spencer. He is evil and only using you." "I mean someday when I do get married," replies Cassie. "Spence is so wonderful; how can he be what you are telling me." "They are good at manipulation and deceit," says Heather. "How can he have so many women begging to be on his side and wanting him if he is evil," asks Cassie. Heather replies, "Because he is using his extremely charming good looks and all his tools on his belt to his advantage in a world where women yearn to feel loved, appreciated, and needed." Cassie couldn't argue or deny any of the facts Heather just listed off to her, for she knew it was true. "What are we supposed to do now asked Penelope?" Heather began by saying, "He isn't only a Fallen Angel sent by Smitty; he is also a shapeshifter that can shift at will and camouflage himself into his surroundings." Cassie got a very scared look on her face as Heather grabbed her hand to console her. "Everyone must play along that everything is good, and that means you mother and you, Cassie. Spencer must think that you both are completely unaware of the situation and don't know what he is. Neither of you can see his malicious Shine so that will help you both. The rest of us can see it, and so that complicates acting normal with that dark glow surrounding him. He already knows we know who he is and why he is here. As for you two, stay calm and act normal." Cassie holds up her hand to Heather and says, "How am I supposed to be intimate with him now? He will expect that because that's normal." Heather replies, "Play his game, Cassie; tell him you have your period. His focus is getting more on his revenge than on you, so you should be fine." Heather knowing that wasn't the full truth, had to keep her sister calm. "Nanook confirmed to me at the store his ability to shapeshift," says Heather. Cassie then gets goosebumps and says, "Creepy old Eskimo is part of this." "Yes, Cassie, he is old, and he is an Eskimo, but he's not creepy, and he is very much a part of this," replies Heather. Heather tells Penelope and Cassie about Nanook and how he is an Inuit Shaman, which basically is what Heather is in his culture. Not exactly, but very close in nature. Cassie is beyond overwhelmed with all the information she was expected to process and digest in such a short amount of time and all at once. She then asks Heather, "What does Spencer shapeshift into?" Heather tells Cassie that Nanook thinks he will shape-shift into a black wolf on the Christmas Eve full moon. Cassie then replies, "Is he a werewolf too?" Heather than can't help it and laughs, "Saying, well, no, not really, he's a Fallen Angel with shape-shifting abilities. According to Nanook, full moons seem to assist him in his power, so that part, yes. Heather than grabs the ivory-carved baby seal dangling around her neck, thinking about Nanook. Penelope notices it an says that's beautiful, Heather. Thank you, Nanook carved it and gave it to me as a gift. It was his way of telling me he could see my Shine. Cassie than says what do you mean? Heather begins to tell Cassie the meaning behind the gift. Baby seals to the Inuit people represent innocence, and they replace the word lamb in the bible with the word seal. Heather tried to explain to Penelope and Cassie that Nanook was telling her that he could see the Shine and that she was a seal sent from the Gods. None of them felt like making cookies after that; instead, all three of them sat in front of the fire with the two Frenchies and reflected. Although they were sitting together, each pondered in different thoughts, with the fire crackling back as if to answer all of life's grand questions.

CHAPTER 27

The sound of the snow machines was the only thing that woke the three women up from their day dreams amongst the flames and crackles. They all looked at each other and knew that act one of the plays was to begin. Dean entered the room first and instantly knew that Heather and Penelope had told Cassie everything; he could tell by the look on Cassie's face. She was looking at him differently now, not in a bad way, but most certainly different. Asher, Cruz, and Grayson entered the cabin, taking off their boots, and they were instantly aware of the look on Heather's face. Spencer walked through the door last, and now everyone was staring at him with the same "We know" look. He says, "What, you didn't think I would come back alive? You didn't think getting rid of me would be that easy, did you, ladies?" Cassie, being a much better actress than Spencer ever gave her credit for, runs to him and hugs him as if nothing had changed while he was gone. Penelope then says she is going to head to bed; it's been a long day, and retreats to her bedroom to have a good cry about her life and its results. The quilted pillow case is damp before she drifts off into a deep sleep. Cassie and Spencer head to bed shortly after that, hand in hand as usual, and Heather is impressed with Cassie's acting abilities. Dean and their three sons join Heather and the Frenchies at the fireplace to warm their bodies, chilled to the bone from the adventure up the mountain. Dean was a man of few words and didn't say much more that evening as Asher told Heather all about the wolf tracks and how they had migrated closer to Nome. The unspoken language was something Heather and the boys had gotten unwantedly used to with Dean. His visions controlled most of his life as a Seer, and that made it tough for others around him to understand him and connect with him. Somethings in life are just not ever meant to be understood, and Dean was one of those things. Heather wasn't sure what the adventure with Spencer was all about that day, but she trusted that Dean had his reasons, and so she left it lay. All the boys eventually retreated into their nightly slumber, leaving Dean and Heather alone in the dark with just the fire illuminating the room. They didn't hear the normal giggling and laughing from Cassie and Spencer's room that night. The cabin had a chill of silence, almost like the calm before the storm. Enjoying wisps of happiness was something Heather regaled in; they were few and far between in her life as a Guardian Angel, so she absorbed these moments like a sponge. Dean could always tell from the look in her eyes that she was distantly somewhere else when she was at her happiest. Being divine doesn't mean constant and complete happiness; it's actually the exact opposite. Guardian Angels absorb all the pain and anguish around them more than the actual person that is experiencing it first-hand. Then it stays with them forever; they house it in their souls. The ones with abilities like Guardians, Seers, and Shaman all have lives of solitude, unexplainable feelings, and unwanted truth by others. This makes them alone and isolated with knowledge and within their own acceptance. Dean kissed Heather on the top of her head and said try to get some rest, dear. He then left the room, leaving Heather being the last of the Mohicans alone with the crackle. Heather enjoyed her time in the quiet alone; this was where she did her best work at healing her soul and preparing herself for the next task at hand. She was almost certain that Spencer was her assignment that she had been waiting for all these years; it wasn't Smitty like she had originally thought. Spencer was going to be a different task all together with his shape-shifting abilities. Nanook was on edge like she had never seen him before. This made Heather feel uneasy and unprepared for the upcoming battle with Spencer, the Fallen Angel, and shape-shifting Demon.

CHAPTER 28

Christmas Eve was upon the Summers, and everyone was on edge with the knowledge of the full moon and Spencer. Spencer made sure to point out to everyone that it was a full moon and Christmas; "What an irony," he stated with a chuckle. Heather had removed Violet's Archangel Blade from its hiding place and was now it resting under her pillow when she slept at night. The Angel Blade was so sharp it was cutting the back of the pillow, spilling white goose down feathers on the floor all around Heather. She felt as though it was her grandmother telling her she was by her side. Violet had the most glorious and stunning gold-gilded grey wings. Heather's son Grayson also had gold-gilded grey wings like his great-grandmother. It almost seemed like they had been a gift to Grayson from Violet when he was fighting for his life as a premature infant. They looked as though they were protecting him like a shield and keeping him safe and warm as they gently rested on his little back in the NICU unit. Dean awoke that morning to white feathers all around Heather, and he knew the Blade was close. He removed a tiny white feather from Heather's forehead and said good morning, Angel. They could hear the commotion downstairs and decided it was time to face reality and get on with their day. As they joined everyone downstairs, Spencer was cooking breakfast. Cassie and Penelope had coffee cups in their hands as they chatted with Asher, Cruz, and Grayson about their trawling adventures on the Bering Sea. The three boys argued about who caught the biggest crab and how Asher's didn't count. For a moment, all was right with the world as Heather watched her family smiling and enjoying each other at the table. Just then, Spencer chimes in with, "Well, Heather looks like your late to the party," with his irritating laugh and wearing her kitchen apron. Dean says to Spencer, "You are mistaken; Heather is the life of the party, Spencer," as he pours himself a much-needed cup of coffee. Everyone went on with the morning as if nothing was on the agenda, and Spencer was extremely happy and in a very suspicious good mood. Heather knew that the full moon was upon them and Spencer would appear as a wolf, but when? Then there was a knock at the door. Heather couldn't imagine who it could be, the cabin was remote, and they very seldom had visitors. As she opened the door, she saw Nanook the Shaman standing in a Christmas sweater with a moose design on the chest, and he was holding a basket of goodies. "Merry Christmas, Heather," he said and, without invitation, began to walk inside the cabin and take off his boots. Heather gives him a big hug and welcomes him to their home, which he had never been to before. Dean and all the boys come around the corner and greet Nanook with hugs and smiles, saying welcome old man, we are glad you're here. Penelope gives Nanook a hug and says Merry Christmas. Cassie then comes around the corner, nervous and intimidated by Nanook, but forces herself to hug him and welcome him. The only person not in the living room greeting Nanook was Spencer. Soon, he appears out of the kitchen, now somber and not in his happy-go-lucky mood he was showing off just moments prior to Nanook's arrival. Everyone in the room becomes silent as Spencer walks over to Nanook. He doesn't hug Nanook and doesn't even shake his hand. he just says, "Well, what a nice surprise." Nanook replies with only a nod at Spencer, and their eyes have conversations without dialog in front of everyone standing there. Spencer seemed to stay back further than what most people would from Nanook. Nanook then turns to Heather and says in his deep yet tender voice, I hope you don't mind if I join you for your celebration. Dean chimed in, not at all. We are glad you came, Nanook. Heather then hugs Nanook one more time and whispers in his ear, "Tootega." Tootega means to walk on water in the Inuit language. Nanook smiles at Heather for only the second time in his life, nodding yes. Spencer, seething with hate over this unwanted house guest, there to disrupt his evil plot, returns to the kitchen alone.

CHAPTER 29

Spencer now has to redo his original plan and is unhappy about the change in his circumstances. He slams the apron down on the counter in disgust. He begins to rethink his strategy, for he knows that another soldier against his immoral crusade has now arrived, and this one is familiar with his shape-shifting capabilities. Spencer was aware that Nanook knew what to look for and would hinder his ultimate end game. Nanook was an interesting Inuit with lots of legends and stories to tell about his culture and traditions. They all sat listening intently to Nanook as he told stories about his father and his grand polar bear legacy. He went on to tell them all about his first hunt with his father and the respect they had to pay to the animals they harvested. It was as though this was the first and last time that Nanook would ever tell his autobiography. Heather asked Nanook if it was alright if she wrote down some of his stories in her journal. He smiled and was honored. The room was in such fascination with Nanook's life and traditions they almost forgot about Spencer, who was still in the Kitchen by himself, sitting at the table alone. Cassie yelled for Spencer to come and join them, and he said he was reading and was fine where he was. Nanook, without hesitation, continued to regale in the hunting story about his first seal and how the hunters would share it with the entire tribe, making it a celebration of life. The Inuit culture is so humbling and grateful for all they are given in life, something other cultures could definitely learn from. The amount of respect that is shown by the hunters to the animals is indescribably beautiful. The appreciation that the culture has for all living things is divine in itself. The Summers, Penelope, and Cassie are in awe of his gratitude to his people and the animals. As a Shaman and one of the highest levels of the tribal high Anarchy, Nanook was still so very vulnerable and modest. Maybe that's the key in life; staying vulnerable is the strongest thing a person can do. Sounds silly, but just maybe. To most people being vulnerable is a sign of weakness; well, maybe it's been the exact opposite all along. Being able to display vulnerability actually demonstrates how strong a person is, to not be afraid, and that is where courage actually lies at its strongest. Nanook was living proof, for he was one of the strongest people that the Summers had ever met.

CHAPTER 30

Nanook told his stories for hours, which seemed like only minutes to his audience, the Summers, Penelope, and Cassie. One story he never told them was about Ahnah, her son, and the night at the trapper's cabin. That was something that he would go to his grave with for the sake of her safety. He also didn't stay long on the subject of his wife; although he mentioned her and how she passed, he soon changed the subject. Heather could see how painful it was for him to talk about her. The most important person in his life, and he couldn't save her. Heather made everyone hot chocolate, and Spencer watched her as she passed by him going to and from the kitchen. The turkey had been roasting in the oven since breakfast and was starting to fill the cabin with the scrumptious aromas of Christmas. Asher, Cruz, and Grayson were teaching Nanook how to make the perfect smores; as they called it, he had never had one before and thought they were overrated. Heather could tell by the first bite he took that he was confused at the combination but made everyone laugh by his facial expressions. It was so nice for Heather to see Nanook among friends and enjoying himself. He knew the impending danger that awaited in the kitchen, and yet she had never seen him so relaxed and ok with the situation. Maybe it was due to all the tragedy and trauma he had witnessed in his life that made him numb to things that were simply out of his control. Either way, it amazed Heather and gave her a sense of peace among all the chaos. Nanook joining her and her family on Christmas was the best gift she would receive that year and one she would cherish for years to come. This would be a Christmas that she wouldn't forget for more reasons than one. Heather made sure to write fast as Nanook spoke; she would even draw little pictures of the hunting weapons and things that his tribe would hand-make and how they would make them. She didn't want to forget a single detail. It was all so interesting and fascinating. She wasn't sure what made her want to write it all down and document what Nanook was telling them, but regardless she did. The things he was revealing to them he had never shared with anyone else his entire life. Shamans are very private people. They are mostly isolated from the tribe and feared. Although greatly respected by all the members holding the highest title within the tribe, they are just a mystery to most and therefore are kept at an arm's length distance. Nanook's wife was treated the same; it just came with the territory of being married to the mysterious Shaman. That gave her a lonely life with Nanook, but she never seemed to mind, was what Nanook felt. Her name was Anji. The Inuit word for grace. Anji lived her life as so, with grace and humility, until she passed. Anji took her position in the tribe very seriously. Being the Shaman's wife, it was her responsibility to love and care for him. No one else would. She did this with grace. She didn't have an easy life as she was orphaned as a child, her mother died in childbirth, and her father was killed in one of the tribe's bear hunts. She was raised by a family friend who took her in and fed and clothed her, but that was about it. She was more of a burden on them as food was scarce, and they had three children of their own to feed and clothe. Her dad was a great hunter with many successful seasons, but the polar bear decided it was time his season was over. Nanook's dad ended up killing that polar bear the next season and always said it was a gift from Anji's dad. Nanook and Anji grew up together and were friends long before they were betrothed. In the Inuit tradition, they practiced child betrothal, meaning it was customary to pledge their children to a future marriage. This was a rite practiced by the Inuit tribes in their society. Anji had been betrothed by her father before he passed to Nanook's father as a gift to his first-born son. The children of two of the most respected hunters in the tribe betrothed only seemed fitting. The dads were correct and got it right.

CHAPTER 31

After a few hours of stories, Nanook removed the Frenchie from his lap and asked everyone where Spencer was. Everyone pointed to the kitchen, and Nanook made his way over there. He was walking slower these days with a bit of an arch in his worn-out back that made him look hunched over from all the miles he had put on his worn-out Shaman body. As he approached Spencer, he looked over his book and took off his glasses, watching Nanook approach him from the living room. Nanook aggressively grabbed the book in Spencer's hand and tossed it to the other side of the table. With everyone watching, Spencer just laughs and says can I help you with something, old man? Nanook leans down and whispers something quietly to Spencer, so quietly only Spencer can hear what was said to him. Dean stands up from the slumber he was in, along with Heather. Asher, Cruz, and

Grayson see their mother standing and join her. The manner in which Dean was standing spoke threats were being made without action. This moment was all too clear, for Dean had seen this moment begin in his vision months prior. As soon as Nanook tossed Spencer's book, Dean knew it was time. The game was about to end. Spencer rose up from his chair, now towering over Nanook about six inches, and looking down at him. Nanook slowly turned around and headed for the front door; Penelope began to say you don't have to leave when Heather motioned to her mother to be quiet and remain where she was on the couch. Spencer followed Nanook, and as fast as they headed to the door, they were gone, and the door was closed. Asher, Cruz, and Grayson were waiting for the word from their mother what their next move needed to be. Heather then hears a vicious growling like sound coming from outside. She motions for her sons to follow her outside. When they reached the deck, they saw Nanook in his armor, and he was standing in front of one of the largest Grizzly Bears they had ever seen. He was shaggy and skinny, looking like he just came out of hibernation, but way too early. Dean soon followed Heather and his sons outside to see the bear facing off with Nanook; it was actually the same bear he had come across that day by the river that had allowed him to live. Only the bear looked different; he didn't have the dark threatening eyes Dean had remembered; instead, he had bright glaring red eyes. Heather stopped Dean as he tried to join Nanook in the snow down below. As Heather grabbed Dean's arm and pulled him back towards her, Dean felt something in her sweater pocket. Heather was wearing a long sweater that went to the floor and had deep pockets in it. Deep enough pockets to hold a wrapped-up Archangel Blade. Dean's eyes got big, and he knew that he had to sit this one out this time, for his visions also confirmed this to him. Dean stepped behind his three sons and brought Penelope and Cassie back inside with their hands over their mouths in shock. That left Heather, Grayson, Cruz, and Asher standing alone on the deck with Nanook and the man-eating bear facing off in front of them. The bear let out the most horrific of all growls, deeper and meaner than what Grizzly Bears normally sound like. Nanook was now putting on his giant mask and gloves that he had placed on the front porch before entering the cabin when he first had arrived. This only angered the bear more, and the bear began to foam and spit, stomping his foot in the snow and leaving his warning tracks with profound claw marks. His razor-sharp claws were at least three inches long and ready to tear open flesh in a matter of seconds. Nanook started his Shaman ceremony prayers and songs as the bear started to sway his neck back in forth in pure rage. The constant swaying was causing the hump on his back to move his chocolate-brown fur to flow forward in a motion that almost mimicked a wave. Nanook takes three steps forward, and the bear takes that as an imminent challenge and also lunges himself three steps forward. They all know, standing stiff and cold on the front porch, that the bear is no bear at all, but this bear was Spencer, who had shape-shifted into a man-eating Grizzly Bear.

CHAPTER 32

Nanook was correct about Spencer being a shape-shifting Demon, but he assumed he would appear as a black wolf on the full moon. Meanwhile, Dean is inside the cabin with Penelope and Cassie, trying to calm them down and reassure them that Nanook, Heather, and the three boys can handle this, and please try to remain calm. Not a trait the Smith women were particularly good at mastering, and reminding them of this only made them more hyper. Never tell a woman to calm down, especially a Smith woman. Dean yells, "Just sit down and don't move," to the two ladies and joins Heather back on the porch. Dean knows the ending to this scene, for he had seen this in one of his visions. He never shared the outcome of this vision with anyone. Heather slowly removes the Archangel Blade from her pocket in order to not draw attention to herself or the blade. It was wrapped

165

in a towel and had already started to cut through; it was so sharp on three sides. Heather leaves the towel in her pocket, only exposing the blade's handle to Dean, Cruz, Grayson, and Asher. They all look down and see the handle of Violet's Archangel Blade and know that was a sign from Heather to get ready. The four of them slowly slid to Heather's side to form a straight line across the porch. This was their front line, and they were ready to charge into battle at the first sign Heather gave them. Nanook was keeping the bear at bay with his prayers and songs, but Heather could see him weakening in strength. It was taking all he had. The bear could also see Nanook weakening in stature and took advantage of the moment, charged swiping Nanook's leg wide open; blood was pouring all around in the snow below. One of Nanook's ivory piercing gloves had penetrated the bear's neck, and the bear let out the most echoing of all growls in pain. Nanook managed to stand up, leaving his glove stuck deep into the bear's massive chest. Nanook was badly hurt, and the blood presenting itself, making the snow bright red was evidence. Heather fully removed the Archangel Blade from her pocket at that moment, giving the four men on the porch the signal it was go time. Heather and her four soldiers descended off the deck in unison, keeping their straight line. The bear is now distracted by the divine line approaching him, and therefore, Nanook is able to back away, holding his wounded leg. The five of them surround the bear on all sides in a circle. He does not like this one bit, and now wounded and bleeding begins to snap his jaws clenching his teeth together, making a horrific grinding sound. The bear sees the Archangel Blade in Heather's hand and looks at all the divine Angels surrounding him. Nanook is back up on his feet and joins the circle that the bear has been trapped in. Cassie and Penelope didn't listen to Dean, of course, and are now both standing on the front porch in silence and disbelief at what they are witnessing. Heather is holding the blade in her right hand with the blade pointing straight down, and it's shimmering even though there was no sun that day. Almost as if it was preparing itself for the Demon it was to send back. Just then, the bear falls over from loss of blood and exhaustion.

The thump was loud and made the snow all around him fly up like a small blizzard.

CHAPTER 33

Nanook approaches the bear and shoves it with his foot checking to see if there is any sign of life, and there is not. Nanook takes off his mask and says to Heather, "He has shifted." Just as Nanook says this to Heather, they hear Cassie scream a high-pitched ear-piercing scream. They all turn to see what the commotion on the porch was. There he was, Spencer, standing in the doorway of the cabin behind Cassie and Penelope. Spencer had a butcher's knife to Penelope's throat that he had just sliced wide open horizontally across her neck, laughing. He drops Penelope's limp body as Heather screams, "No," he then shoves the knife into Cassie's belly, hugging her and holding her tight as the knife penetrates deep into her stomach. Spencer then lets go of Cassie as she falls backward on the porch holding the knife in her stomach and coughing up blood. All the meanwhile, he is laughing and eating up every moment of his ruin and destruction. They all rushed to the porch, but it was too late; he had killed both Cassie and Penelope; they were bleeding out in front of them, and help was too far out to arrive in time. Spencer walks down the stairs of the porch, still chuckling and holding the knife, watching Heather closely. He is pleased with himself and thinks he has won the wicked chess match he had been playing with all of them all along. He knew if he shifted into the old bear that Dean was all too familiar with, it would distract Nanook and the rest of them. Nanook should have known that having Spencer join him outside to shift and duel was too easy, and there was another plan in play. For this, he was angry at himself for having been tricked. Spencer underestimating Nanook, thought this is too easy and took on his challenge, thinking he had the upper hand. Spencer was now standing in front of the five of them with a mischievous and arrogant smirk on his face that they all wanted to rip off his lips. Just then, Nanook wanting to make things right and give Heather and her family the best fighting chance charges Spencer with his last ounce of fight in him and his remaining ivory carved glove, and Spencer stabs Nanook in his chest with the butcher's knife. Cruz, on Heather's right side, grabs the blade from Heather's hand and stabs Spencer in his side as hard and fast as he can. There is an enormous burst of light that blinds them all. It's bright, and inside it is a jet-black ball that the light surrounds, begins to engulf, and makes it dissipate, getting brighter and brighter. The particles that begin to fall all around them look like freshly fallen snow on a calm, crisp winter's night. Just as fast as Spencer came into their lives, he was gone. The only thing remaining of him was the devastation he had left behind.

CHAPTER 34

Heather ran inside and dialed 911. It was Christmas Eve, and so the emergency lines were not running at the normal speed of urgency. She ran to her sister and mother to check for a pulse, but Asher and Grayson said, "Mom, they are gone." She couldn't find a pulse on either of them. She then ran to Nanook, where Cruz was kneeling, and Dean was now holding him in his arms. He was barely breathing but was awake. She told Nanook to hold on, to stay strong, and that help was coming. When help arrived, Heather explained to the police with utter sadness in her heart that Cassie's boyfriend, Spencer, from California, had gone insane on her sister and mother, Penelope, and had taken off into the woods. The police put out a 10-54 for possible dead bodies and a 10-72 for the knifing and search for a possible murderer Spencer. Heather found a picture of Spencer on Cassie's phone sitting on the end table, so she could give them one. The police then looked over and saw the dead Grizzly Bear with Nanook's Shaman glove still penetrating the bear's neck, and with a puzzled look on their faces, asked them what the hell happened here? Dean chimes in and says I told you, boys, that this bear was going to try to get the best of me one of these days. Good thing Nanook joined us for Christmas, or I would have been a goner, getting firewood. Dean was friends with the two officers on site, who had heard Dean tell his famous Grizzly Bear encounter and survival story many times, so they didn't push the issue any further. The officers commented how it was so crazy that the bear came out of hibernation and how rare of an occurrence that really is. "Full moon," one officer said to the other officer. Shrugging their shoulders and telling Dean, Man, he really had it out for you, I guess. They gave their condolences to the Summers, took down their statements, and said they were so sorry this had to happen on Christmas Eve of all nights. The ambulance rushed Nanook to the hospital; when he got there, he was placed into emergency surgery for his life-threatening bear wound on his leg and for the knife wound in his chest.

CHAPTER 35

The coroner came and removed Cassie and Penelope's bodies from the front porch. The Summers all joined hands and once again were in a straight line as they watched the lifeless bodies of their loved ones be lifted into body bags. A site none of them ever imagined seeing in their lifetime. Dean had seen the three body bags, but it had never been revealed to him who was in two of those bags. This was one reason why he never shared his visions. Heather and all her sons' pain was unexplainable and untreatable. Guardians' wounds stay open and fresh for their entire lives. Heather stood there with tears rolling down her face. She was devastated, but simultaneously her heart was at peace knowing that Cassie and Penelope had several loved ones waiting for them. She knew that Violet, Horace, Clementine, Cletus, and Autumn would take care of them for her, and it was their turn to love them.

Heather was to remain on this earth to complete an assignment that, once again, she had not yet reached. The agony was like acid being poured into a new cut. Smitty was still causing havoc and chaos even though he was gone, but would he ever truly be gone? Demons are ruthless and relentless creatures that never seem to give up. The Summers rushed to the hospital to be by Nanook's side. The doctors told them he only had a ten percent chance of making it. The leg surgery didn't go as planned, they were able to stop the bleeding, but they had to amputate Nanook's leg. His chest surgery was a four-hour surgery. The knife had missed his heart by three inches but caused some damage around his arteries they had to repair. He was in ICU and was stable for the moment, but no promises, they were told. The Summers, with the heaviest of hearts that they have ever had, returned back to the cabin late that Christmas Eve night. The blood-stained front porch and the blood-soaked snow welcomed them home.

CHAPTER 36

The blood stains were the only remaining traces of Cassie Lane Heather's sister, Penelope Smith Heather's mother, and Spencer Doyle Heather's revenge from Smitty. As they approached the front door, Heather got out the old worn-out skeleton key and began to turn the key when she saw a black shadow out of the corner of her eye. It had bright red piercing eyes and was hiding in the darkness off on the shadowy side of the deck. Just then, it jumps out of the blackness concealing it and grabs Dean by the neck, throwing him back off the deck. The remaining four left standing on the blood-stained deck turn to see Dean pinned on his back. A dark-as-night black wolf was standing on Dean's chest with its massive paws. Dean's neck was bleeding and torn open. When the wolf sees and hears the remaining Summers screaming and rushing off the deck, it sprints into the murky wilderness abyss, only looking back once at Heather. She can only see its bright glaring eyes off in the distance. Everything that Nanook had explained to her about shape-shifting Demons flew through her mind, swirling around and around, but how could this be Spencer was gone? Cruz had stabbed him with Violet's Archangel Blade. He had sent him back to hell, where he came from, where he was left to answer to Smitty. Heather and the boys tried to stop the bleeding as Dean passed right in front of their eyes. They called the police once again, and they were in complete shock that, yet again, they were back at the Summer's cabin for another emergency. They confirmed it was a wolf attack by the marks on Dean and the tracks all around the cabin. They put out a 10-91V to be on the lookout for a vicious rabid lone wolf in the area. They got the DNR to come out and sweep the woods, and they found nothing but bloody wolf tracks that came to an abrupt stop, almost as if they vanished into thin air. The lead had gone cold, and they were left with no answers. They shook their heads and said that full moons make not only people go crazy but animals as well. They figured that all the blood from the murders and the Grizzly Bear must have drawn the pack down from the mountains. They stated that they had seen the pack getting closer and closer to the Nome city limits and that they were afraid something like this would happen. Grayson, Cruz, and Asher confirmed that they, too, had just been up the mountain on the snow machines with Dean and seen the same tracks and fresh kills very close to Nome. The boys knew that would only stop any extra questions from the authorities, but the three of them knew Dean had brought them up there to show them the tracks intentionally. Dean made sure to point out to all three boys that he thought they were coming closer and that the pack had some fresh kills in the area. This was all on purpose; in his own way, he was telling his three sons his fate without actually breaking their hearts before their due time. Heather was beside herself. She not only just lost her mother, Penelope, her sister Cassie, but now her soul mate Dean. She was numb with pain. It tore so deep into her divine soul, but she had to remain strong for her guardian sons. This most certainly would be a Christmas Eve that would tattoo itself in their hearts. Seers have visions and foresee some of the future, but at the same time, it is fate. It's a curse for a Seer to know the future of events, even life, and death, but not be able to change it. They are only allowed to foresee the future, not rearrange the outcomes. A life of complete torment, living with an uninvited crystal ball, was the life of a Seer. That was Dean's life. He had witnessed his own death in his visions and was aware it was going to be by a black wolf. There was no shifting the finish line.

"Three deaths in one family in one night on Christmas Eve," the police officer said with sadness in his voice and tears in his eyes. He was also friends with Dean and the family, so it was also a loss for him. "Why don't you and the boys come into town and stay with my family and me? This is just too much out here, with all this tragedy," as he held his arms out in disgust. Heather looked at her three Shining sons and said to the officer, thank you for the kind offer. We will be just Shine; I mean, fine. Heather heard the phone ringing inside the cabin and excused herself from the police and her statement about the wolf attack on Dean. She stopped only for a moment to reassure the dogs that everything was going to be ok, as they both were very scared and nervous with all the commotion. Once she reached the phone, on the other end of the line was a nurse from the ICU at the hospital in Nome. She was anxiously asking for Heather, explaining how Nanook was awake, upset, and could barely talk but won't stop asking for you. He keeps saying one word over and over again. "Ijiraq, Ijiraq, Ijiraq." Heather stands there still, tremoring from her distress and the sudden and unexpected loss of her husband, Dean. She was then jolted by the information coming from the other end of the phone line. Heather realized what the word meant that Nanook was repeating. Ijiraq means a shapeshifting Demon that kidnaps children and young teens abandons them, and hides them away. They are masters of shapeshifting and can appear as humans, caribou, wolves, or a combination of them all. They can confuse their victims, cast illusions, use magic, and curse their victims to lose their way. The area that they inhabit is always cursed. What Heather was unaware of at the time was that the cabin they were residing in was owned by non-other than the Mayor of Nome. Nanook knew this but kept it all to himself till now. The nurse on the other end of the phone is saying, "Hello, hello, are you there?" "Yes, I am here." Heather says, "Thank you for calling. We will be there as soon as we can." "Oh, there's one more thing that he said," the nurse begins to repeat. Heather is hanging up the phone, thinking the nurse has already hung up on her end. What Heather doesn't hear her say is, "He said you're in grave danger; don't go back to the…" click.

www.ingramcontent.com/pod-product-compliance
Lightning Source LLC
Chambersburg PA
CBHW071951110426
42744CB00030B/759